Dr. G Rajendran

Dedication

I dedicate this book to my late father, Andapuram K. Ganesan, and my late mother, Bagiyam. They taught me to trust in myself, and their blessings will always be a part of who I am. Through this book, I hope to honor their memory and inspire others, just as they have inspired me.

Preface

The purpose of this book, "Unlock Your Key Values," is to help you discover and embrace your core values. By identifying your values, you can align your actions and behaviors with your authentic self, and create a life of meaning, purpose, and fulfillment. This book is not a one-size-fits-all guide, but a tool that encourages you to explore your unique values, and guides you through a process of self-discovery and reflection.

In this book, you will find various exercises, tools, and strategies to help you identify and embrace your key values. You will learn about the importance of values in our lives, and how they can shape our relationships, our careers, and our overall well-being. You will explore the different domains of life, such as personal growth, relationships, work, and spirituality, and how your values can influence each of them.

Whether you are feeling lost, stuck, or unfulfilled in your life, or you simply want to deepen your self-awareness and personal growth, this book is for you. It is a practical guide that will empower you to unlock your key values and live a life of purpose and meaning.

Remember that the journey towards self-discovery is not always easy, but it is worth it. It is a journey of self-compassion, self-acceptance, and self-love. I encourage you to approach this book with an open mind, a curious heart, and a willingness to embrace your true self. May this book guide you towards a life of authenticity, fulfillment, and joy.

Dr. G Rajendran

Introduction

Unlock Key Values is a comprehensive guide to designing a life that aligns with your values and goals. It covers a wide range of topics, from management of key values to education and parenting, health and wealth, and global responsibility.

Part 1, "Managing Key Values," explores the significance of identifying your values and how to manage them effectively. It includes practical advice on how to prioritize your values and align them with your life goals.

Part 2, "Designing Desired Life," focuses on designing a desired life that aligns with your values and goals. It includes practical advice on how to create a vision board, set goals, and develop a roadmap to achieve your desired lifestyle.

Part 3, "Signifying Simplification," discusses the importance of living a simple life and how it can contribute to personal growth and financial freedom. It includes personal stories of how simplifying one's life has led to greater happiness and success.

Part 4, "Educating and Parenting," covers the benefits of education, brain development, and the dos and don'ts for parents. It emphasizes the role of education and parenting in helping children develop key values and achieve their life goals.

Part 5, "Caring Health and Wealth," provides practical advice on maintaining good physical and mental health and managing personal finances to achieve financial freedom. Travel and Ease, discusses the dos and don'ts during travel trips and how travel can contribute to personal growth and greater understanding of different cultures.

Part 6, "Managing Life Style," refers to the conscious and proactive approach to managing one's habits, behavior's, and daily routines to improve health and overall well-being.

Part 7, "Digitizing Life," explores the role of digital technology, artificial intelligence, and innovation in personal growth and financial freedom. It emphasizes the importance of using digital technology wisely and avoiding the pitfalls of excessive digital consumption.

Part 8, "Managing Growth," discusses the dangers of pursuing excessive materialistic growth and the advantages of holistic growth and embracing sustainable growth. It includes preventing global warming and the responsibilities of every individual and corporation.

Finally, Part 9, "Global Caring," emphasizes the importance of global responsibility and how it can contribute to personal growth and financial freedom. It includes practical advice on how to make a positive impact on the world and be a responsible global citizen.

Overall, Unlock Key Values provides practical advice, inspiring stories, and valuable insights into designing a life that aligns with your values and goals. It is a must-read for anyone who wants to live a meaningful life, achieve personal growth and financial freedom, and make a positive impact on the world.

UNLOCK KEY VALUES

to design desired ways

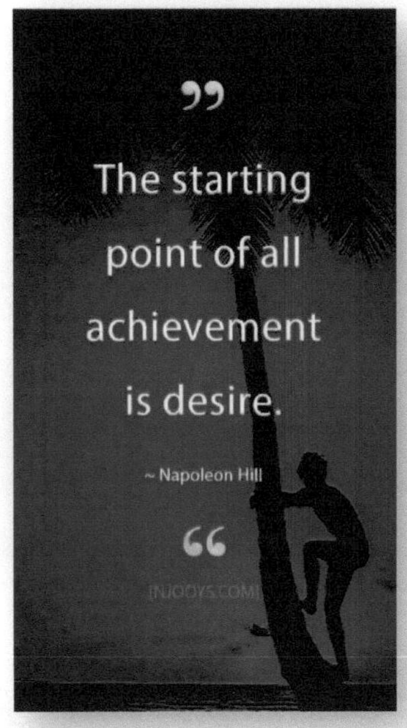

UNLOCK

KEY VALUES

... to design desired ways

“Strive not to be a

Success,

but rather to be of

VALUE”.

Albert Einstein

1. Managing Key Values

The key question is, "Where should we keep the key?"

Key gets its power when it is positioned in an appropriate place for utilization.

A key has to do its job of locking or unlocking. Key does its job when it's available at an appropriate, unlocked place. If the key is kept safely inside a locked area or in an unknown location, it cannot perform its function and is rendered useless. You may call it a key, but it becomes iron when it does not perform its job.

"People say money isn't the key to happiness, but I've always thought that if you have enough money, you can have a key made." - Joan Rivers

The same way, money has its own question: "Where should we keep the money?"

The same way money has to do its job of buying, selling, or engaging in some sort of activity like banking or stocking, it has to circulate like blood. If the money does not do any kind of job, then it becomes mere paper and loses its title "money" to remain as "mere paper" in a real economic sense. If the money is kept safely inside the lockers or not used to do its job, it is not allowed to use its power or value and becomes meaningless paper with the title "money."

The meaning of money varies depending on a person's perspective and life circumstances. Here are a few common meanings of money:

Currency for goods and services: One of the most basic meanings of money is as a means of exchange for goods and services. In this sense, money is simply a tool that allows us to acquire the things we need and want in life.

Status and power: For some people, money represents status and power. Having a lot of money can provide access to opportunities, privileges, and social connections that may not be available to those with less money.

Security and stability: Money can also represent security and stability for many people. Having a steady income and savings can provide a sense of safety and peace of mind, allowing people to plan for the future and feel more in control of their lives.

Freedom and flexibility: Money can also provide freedom and flexibility, allowing people to pursue their interests and passions, travel, and experience new things.

Philanthropy and giving: Charitable giving and philanthropy can be ways to use money to help others and make a difference in the world.

Key Values

Key values are the principles that guide our actions and behaviors in our day-to-day lives. They help us live a life of integrity, purpose, and meaning. Here are some key values that are important for our day-to-day lives:

Honesty: Honesty is the foundation of all relationships, and it is essential for building trust and respect. Being honest with ourselves and others helps us maintain healthy and meaningful relationships and avoid conflicts.

Respect: Respect for others is important in all aspects of our lives. It means treating others with kindness, empathy, and understanding, regardless of their background, beliefs, or values. When we show respect to others, we create a positive environment where everyone feels valued and appreciated.

Responsibility: Responsibility means taking ownership of our actions and being accountable for our decisions. It means being proactive, organized, and reliable in all aspects of our lives. By taking

responsibility for our actions, we can build trust and credibility with others and achieve our goals.

Compassion: Compassion means showing kindness and empathy towards others. It involves being aware of other people's emotions and needs and responding with care and understanding. When we show compassion, we can create positive relationships and make a positive impact on the world.

Perseverance: Perseverance means persisting in the face of challenges and obstacles. It means having the determination to achieve our goals, no matter how difficult they may be. By persevering, we can build resilience, develop our skills, and achieve our dreams.

Gratitude: Gratitude means being thankful for what we have in our lives. It involves acknowledging the good things that we have and being appreciative of the people and experiences that make our lives better. By practicing gratitude, we can cultivate a positive mindset and improve our overall well-being.

Forgiveness: Forgiveness means letting go of anger, resentment, and bitterness towards others. It involves recognizing that people make mistakes and that we all have flaws. By practicing forgiveness, we can release negative emotions, improve our relationships, and move on from past hurt.

These key values are essential for leading a fulfilling and meaningful life. By incorporating these values into our day-to-day lives, we can build strong relationships, achieve our goals, and make a positive impact on the world.

Unlocking Your Power

The power to achieve greatness lies within each and every one of us. However, this power often remains untapped due to various reasons, such as fear, self-doubt, or lack of knowledge. To unlock your power and unleash your full potential, it is crucial to understand and overcome these barriers.

One of the key barriers to unlocking your power is fear. Fear can prevent you from taking risks and pursuing your goals. It is important to remember that fear is a natural

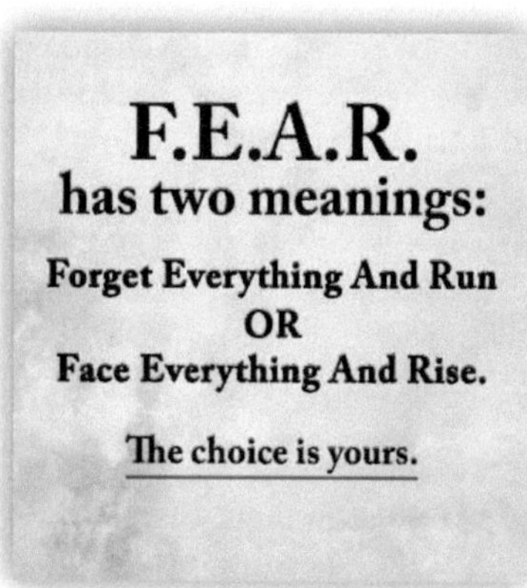

emotion, but it should not control your actions. Instead, acknowledge your fear and use it as motivation to move forward. Identify the root cause of your fear and challenge your negative beliefs. By doing so, you can build your confidence and develop a positive mindset.

Self-doubt is another barrier that can hinder you from unlocking your power. Many people doubt their abilities and question their worth, which can limit their potential.

To overcome self-doubt, it is essential to shift your mindset and focus on your strengths. Celebrate your successes and acknowledge your achievements, no matter how small they may be. Surround yourself with positive influences and seek support from your loved ones. Additionally, never be afraid to ask for help or seek advice from mentors or coaches.

Lack of knowledge is also a barrier that can prevent you from unlocking your power. Knowledge is power, and it is essential to continuously learn and grow. Develop a growth mindset and seek out opportunities to learn new skills or gain new experiences. Attend seminars, read books, take courses, or even start a new hobby. The more knowledge you gain, the more confident you will become and the more power you will have to achieve your goals.

Unlocking your power requires a combination of self-awareness, determination, and a willingness to learn. By overcoming the barriers of fear, self-doubt, and lack of knowledge, you can unleash your full potential and achieve greatness. Remember to always stay true to yourself, set goals that align with your values, and never give up on your dreams.

The power to achieve greatness is within you, waiting to be unlocked.

Being Unique

Each one of us is born with a unique set of talents, skills, and traits that sets us apart from others. Being unique is not only a quality that makes us special; it is also a valuable asset that can contribute to our personal and professional success. However, in a world that often

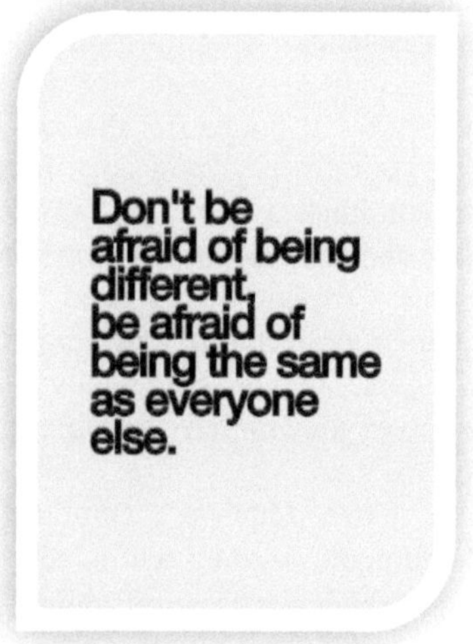

values conformity, being unique can be a challenge. It requires us to embrace our individuality and celebrate our differences.

One of the most important aspects of being unique is embracing our authenticity. This means being true to ourselves, our values, and our beliefs. It can be tempting to conform to societal norms or to please others, but in doing so, we risk losing our true identity. By staying true to ourselves, we can create a sense of purpose and fulfilment that cannot be found by conforming to others' expectations.

Another aspect of being unique is recognizing and cultivating our talents and skills. We all have a unique set of talents and skills that can be honed and developed. By identifying our strengths, we can build upon them and use them to our advantage. This can help us stand out in our personal and professional lives and create a sense of confidence and competence.

Being unique also means embracing our differences and respecting those of others. No two people are exactly the same, and our differences should be celebrated, not judged. By embracing diversity, we can learn from others and gain a broader perspective. This can help us grow and develop, and it can also help us become more empathetic and understanding of others.

In a world that often values conformity and fitting in, being unique can be a challenge. However, by embracing our authenticity, cultivating our talents, and respecting the differences of others, we can create a life that is fulfilling and meaningful. Being unique is not just about being different; it is about celebrating our individuality and using it to create a life that is authentic and true to ourselves.

Human and Money

An individual can live anywhere in the world with a minimum of 30 US dollars per day. Therefore, the ideal amount for an individual to live anywhere in the world is an average of 10,000 US dollars per year. However, if you calculate the cost for living for 100 years in any part of the world, it comes to one million US dollars In conclusion, one would need to have one million dollars to live comfortably for 100 years anywhere in the world.

We only have 10 years of our lives to enjoy and fulfill our desires. The logical truth is that we cannot control the first 15 years and last 15 years. The remaining 70 years include 8 hours of sleep per day, which amounts to one-third of 70, or 23 years. Work time, including 10 hours of commuting per day, takes out nearly 20 years of the remaining 47 years. Out of the 27 years left, daily essential obligations such as showering, grooming, dining, and others take an average of 3 hours per day, which amounts to one-eighth of 27 years, or 3 years. Attending essential family functions, traveling, shopping, hospitalization, sickness, repairs and maintenance of household things and personal accessories, natural calamities, untoward incidents, floods, power shut down, transport, and others take out nearly 14 years. Therefore, we have only 10 years left to design our desired life, subject to the consideration of living for 100 years.

Money plays an important role in human life, as it provides a means to obtain basic necessities, such as food, shelter, and clothing, and to achieve higher goals and

> "Values are like fingerprints. Nobody's are the same, but you leave them all over everything you do."

aspirations. However, it is important to maintain a healthy relationship with money, as it can also lead to negative consequences such as stress, greed, and materialism. When it comes to money, it is important to strike a balance between meeting our basic needs and pursuing our goals and aspirations. We should focus on earning money in a way that aligns with our personal values and beliefs and use it in a way that supports our well-being and the well-being of others.

It is important to avoid becoming overly attached to money or defining our self-worth based on our financial status. We should focus on cultivating positive relationships, finding purpose and meaning in our lives, and pursuing our passions and interests rather than simply accumulating wealth.

Money can be viewed as an objective measure of value as it serves as a medium of exchange for goods and services. It is a tool that can be used to facilitate economic transactions and is generally accepted as a form of payment. In this sense, money can be seen as objective, as it has a universally recognized value and is not dependent on personal opinions or values.

However, the role of money in society and its value are not completely objective. The value of money is determined by a variety of factors, including supply and demand, inflation, interest rates, and government policies. These factors can fluctuate and change over time, leading to changes in the value of money.

Life and the future are inherently interconnected, as the decisions we make and the actions we take in the present can significantly impact our future. It's important to take a long-term perspective when considering our goals and plans, as well as the potential consequences of our choices.

One way to approach life and the future is to set clear goals and work towards them incrementally over time. This can involve identifying what is most important to you, both in terms of your personal and professional life, and then creating a plan to achieve those goals.

It's also important to remain open to change and adapt to new circumstances as they arise, as the future is inherently unpredictable. Being flexible and resilient can help us navigate unexpected challenges and take advantage of new opportunities.

Moreover, it's important to prioritize self-care and well-being, as these can significantly impact our ability to achieve our goals and live a fulfilling life. If we keep on doing what we are always doing, then we will keep on getting what we have been always getting. This can involve cultivating new relationships, engaging differently and doing things from out of our own comfort zone.

We have been taught right from home, school and everywhere on how to save money but failed to teach how to spend the saved money wisely. Our thought process always played to make money and to save for future. However, failed to understand the purpose of the hard earned money to make our present life healthier and happier.

Using money wisely means managing it in a way that helps you achieve your financial goals while also supporting your overall well-being. Some strategies for using money wisely include:

Creating a budget: Establish a budget that outlines your income and expenses, and stick to it. This can help you avoid overspending and keep your finances on track.

Saving for the future: Set aside money for emergencies and for long-term goals, such as retirement or buying a house. This can help you achieve financial stability and security.

Avoiding debt: Try to avoid taking on too much debt or using credit cards to finance purchases that you can't afford. High levels of debt can lead to financial stress and strain.

Investing in yourself: Use your money to invest in yourself, such as by pursuing education or training that can improve your earning potential or help you achieve your goals.

Giving back: Consider donating a portion of your income to causes or organizations that you care about. This can help you feel more fulfilled and make a positive impact on the world.

By using money wisely, you can achieve your financial goals while also supporting your overall well-being and making a positive impact on the world.

The meaning of money varies depending on a person's values and life circumstances. It can represent currency for goods and services, status and power, security and stability, freedom and flexibility, or philanthropy and giving. Understanding the meaning of money can help individuals make better decisions about how to earn, spend, and manage their finances.

You Are Your Own Guru

In our search for guidance and enlightenment, we often look to external sources for answers. We may seek the advice of spiritual leaders, self-help gurus, or even turn to religion to find meaning and purpose in our lives. However, the truth is that the greatest source of wisdom lies within ourselves. We are our own gurus.

To be our own guru means to take ownership of our lives and be responsible for our own growth and development. It means recognizing our innate wisdom and listening to our inner voice. We each have a unique journey, and only we know what is best for ourselves. It is important to trust ourselves and our instincts and to have the courage to follow our own path.

Being your own guru requires self-awareness and introspection. It means taking the time to reflect on our thoughts, emotions, and actions. Through self-reflection, we can gain clarity and understanding of our beliefs, values, and purpose. We can identify our strengths and weaknesses and work towards becoming the best version of ourselves.

It is also important to cultivate a daily practice that supports our growth and development. This may include meditation, journaling, yoga, or any other practice that brings us inner peace and clarity. Through regular practice, we can connect with our inner selves and gain a deeper understanding of our purpose and direction.

Being your own guru does not mean that we should reject external sources of guidance and inspiration. It simply means that we should be discerning in our approach and trust our own intuition. We can learn from others and be inspired by their wisdom, but ultimately, the answers lie within us.

The idea of being your own guru is empowering and liberating. It reminds us that we have the power to create our own destiny and live a life of purpose and fulfillment. We are our own greatest teachers, and the journey of self-discovery is one of the most rewarding experiences we can have. By trusting ourselves and our inner voice, we can unlock our full potential and create a life of meaning and joy

Being Truthful

Our conscience is a powerful internal voice that guides us towards what is right and wrong. It is a moral compass that helps us make decisions and navigate through life's challenges. However, in order to live in alignment with our conscience, we must be truthful to ourselves.

This means being honest about our thoughts, feelings, and actions and taking responsibility for our choices. Being true to one's self-conscience necessitates self-reflection and introspection. It means taking the time to examine our values, beliefs, and motivations. We must ask ourselves tough questions and be willing to face the answers, even if they are uncomfortable. This can be a difficult process, but it is essential for personal growth and development.

Being truthful to one's self also means being accountable for our actions. We must take responsibility for our choices and the consequences that follow. This can be challenging, as it requires humility and the willingness to admit our mistakes. However, by being accountable, we can learn from our mistakes and make better choices in the future.

In order to live in alignment with our conscience, we must also be true to our authentic selves. This means being honest about who we are and what we want in life. It can be tempting to conform to societal norms or to please others, but in doing so, we risk losing our true identity. By staying true to ourselves, we can create a sense of purpose and fulfilment that cannot be found by conforming to others' expectations.

Living in alignment with our conscience requires courage and a commitment to personal growth. It requires us to be honest with ourselves, take responsibility for our choices, and stay true to our authentic selves. While this may be a challenging journey, it is one that can lead to a life of purpose, fulfilment, and inner peace. By being truthful to our self-conscience, we can create a life that is true to our values, beliefs, and aspirations.

“You were born

an original

don’t die a copy”.

2. Designing Desired Life

Designing a desired life means creating a vision for the

life you want to live and taking intentional steps to bring that vision to fruition. Here are some steps you can take to design a desired life:

We all have a vision of what our ideal life should look like, but very often, we get bogged down by our daily struggles and forget to pursue our dreams.

Living the life, we desire is not just about material possessions or external achievements. It's about finding meaning, purpose, and fulfilment in our lives. It's about living a life that aligns with our deepest values and desires. It's about creating a life that makes us truly happy and content

"Teach design, and you will design the future."

You have the power to create the life that you desire. The starting point of all achievement is desire. Desires, interests, or ambitions to achieve in your life will be managed scientifically, digitally, and diligently to the optimum level, subject to a minimum level of sources.

All creatures have designs. Design is blended with all kinds of civilization and reflected in different modes. The historical evidence proves that during the Stone Age itself, they designed stones to use for different purposes to survive. Design is a form of simplification. Anything without design will not be much use for any particular task or job. The objectivity of design is to achieve your desired result using the critical path method. Design redefines the concept of connecting one point to another point from A to B in a straight line or using a complex method.

Human life also has two points: birth and death. Our lives are linked by two events: birth and death. Birth and death are linear processes. There are differences between living and existing. Merely existing shows life as a straight line; it is a normal process with no curves or abnormal patterns. So those people come under the category of existence.

Living with Design

We design our temples or decorate our houses with designs like *kolam*, art, sculpture, portraits, etc. However, we fail to design our own lives. We give names to our babies, but we fail to create fame for them by creating a desired life for them. Instead, we impose our desires and unfulfillment on them in all walks of life to make a straight line of end points like everyone else. As a result, preconceived knowledge, a conditioned mind, and limited freedom make our lives difficult from birth. Freedom is a birthright, and it manifests itself in all aspects of our lives. It starts with a free mind, freedom to choose, freedom to speak, freedom to pursue their own interests, etc. True self-control is freedom. Be yourself, because an original is worth more than a copy.

We seldom give importance to design, aesthetic values, and the significance of products in our day-to-day usage. There are so many ways we fail to understand reality and ignore artistic values, which are integrated with many stimulating factors for our brain and our well-being. Book cover design, in general, carries the message of the book's content. The book covers alone accounts for nearly one-fourth of the book's cost because of many factors like design, color reproduction, high GSM art paper, etc. However, we typically use a brown color wrapper to cover the entire book cover, hiding all aesthetic values of the book while also losing one-fourth of the book's cost. The same way we used to cover our mobiles, suitcases, TVs, etc., this is a waste of our money because all these products have been heavily marketed for their look and feel.

The same way automobile companies spend millions and millions of dollars on the look and feel of aesthetic values without any compromise on aerodynamics and safety. However, we tend to fix extra fittings contrary to the aerodynamics and safety parameters of the vehicle and lose not only money but also our lives.

We should say "no" to wrappers on any text book or any book or workbook because wrapping up is nothing but

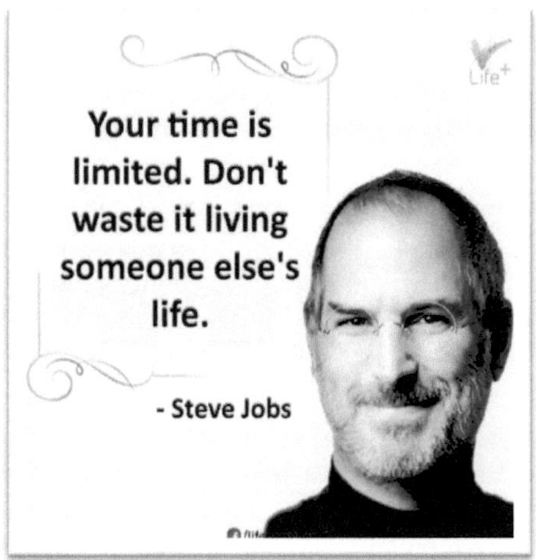

wrapping our brain to halt our creativity. Desire is to identify what we truly want. We need to get clear on our goals, our passions, and our values. When we have a clear picture of what we want, we can then create a roadmap that will help us achieve our goals. It's not enough to just have a plan; we need to put in the work and make things happen. We need to take small, actionable steps every day that will move us closer to our desired life. We need to stay committed to our vision. We will face challenges, setbacks, and obstacles along the way, but we must keep our eyes on the prize and never give up. We need to believe in ourselves, stay focused, and keep pushing forward until we achieve our goals.

Designing and achieving your desired life is a personal journey that requires self-reflection, goal-setting, and action. Here are some tips for creating the life you desire:

Identify your values: Take time to identify your core values and what matters most to you. This can help you prioritize what's important and make decisions that align with your values.

Set goals: Create clear and specific goals for your personal and professional life. This can help you stay motivated and focused on your path to success.

Create a plan: Develop a plan to achieve your goals, including the steps you need to take and the resources you need to get there.

Take action: Take consistent and intentional action towards your goals. This can help you build momentum and move closer to achieving your desired life.

Seek support. Surround yourself with positive and supportive people who can encourage and inspire you on your journey. Consider working with a coach or mentor to help you stay on track and overcome obstacles.

Achieving your desired life requires commitment, focus, and perseverance. By identifying your values, setting goals, creating a plan, taking action, and seeking support, you can design the life you desire and live a fulfilling and meaningful life.

Designing your life refers to taking a proactive and intentional approach to creating a life that aligns with your values, goals, and aspirations. It involves setting clear and meaningful objectives and making deliberate choices to help you achieve them.

Design is an Art of Life

“Design is where science and art break even.”

"You are the artist of your own life." Don’t hand the paintbrush to anyone else." – Blebillion

You are free to be who you were created to be. While the world will do its best to define you, telling you who to be, how to act, and what to think, remember: every fiber of your being was designed with purpose. The way you think, communicate ideas, and express yourself—it is a unique and electric combination that no one else has.

Too often, we misconstrue the evolution of life. We buy into the idea that we must "become" someone to be great. But greatness is already in us. It’s at the core of who we are. The challenge is to not strive to become something else but instead uncover the greatness already within us.

Our power lies not in becoming someone else but in unfolding and revealing to the world who we have been created to be. So, give yourself permission to unfold, stripping down to the rawest and most authentic version of yourself and seeing it as brilliant and valuable. As you do, you will begin to see yourself living freely and glowing with light, allowing you to experience the greatness you were destined for.

Create your life at an early stage in order to achieve or meet your life's goal. The main purpose is to live happily and promote peaceful human coexistence and to make our world safe for all living things.

Desire or wanting something, especially strongly or wishfully, is the emotion of longing for the goal. Millions of permutations and combinations result in life. In a recent talk at TEDx San Francisco, Mel Robbins mentioned that scientists estimate the probability of your being born at about one in 400 trillion. Life is very precious, and every one of us has a unique way to represent our lives with purpose.

Designing Life Involves

Self-reflection: Take time to understand your values, priorities, and goals. Ask yourself what kind of life you want to live and what you want to accomplish.

Prioritizing: Make a list of your priorities and focus on the most important ones first.

Planning: Create a roadmap for how you'll achieve your goals and make sure your daily habits and routines support your desired outcomes.

Taking action: Start taking steps towards your goals, no matter how small. Remember that progress, not perfection, is the goal.

Adapting: Be open to change and be prepared to adjust your plan as needed. Life is unpredictable, so be flexible and willing to make modifications.

Designing your life is an ongoing process, and it takes effort, determination, and resilience. But with dedication, you can create a life that is fulfilling, meaningful, and in line with your personal values and goals.

We can create a fulfilling and meaningful existence that aligns with your values, goals, and aspirations.

A desired lifestyle is not just about material possessions

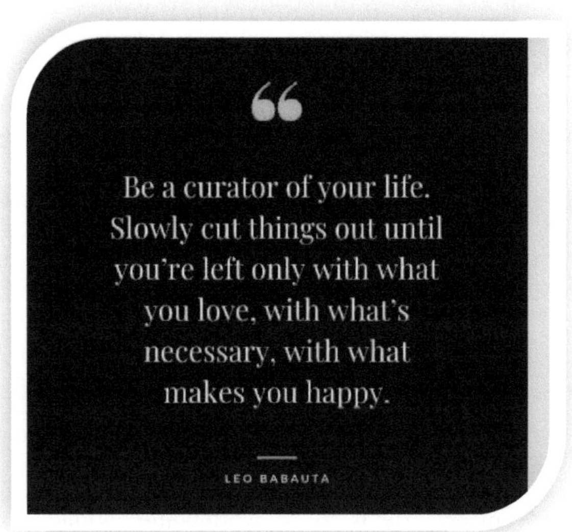

or external achievements. It is about cultivating inner peace, joy, and fulfillment. It involves making intentional choices that align with our values and goals and taking steps towards personal growth and development.

In this book, we have explored various aspects of a desired lifestyle, including healthy habits, meaningful relationships, financial management, personal growth, and mindfulness. By incorporating these principles into our lives, we can create a life of purpose, happiness, and fulfilment.

Remember that the journey towards a desired lifestyle is unique for everyone. It is important to set realistic goals, stay committed to our values, and embrace the process with patience and self-compassion. With dedication and perseverance, we can create the life we truly desire and deserve.

In conclusion, adopting a desired lifestyle is an ongoing journey that requires continuous effort and self-reflection. It is a way of life that emphasizes living with intention, purpose, and mindfulness. By prioritizing our physical, mental, and emotional well-being, we can improve our quality of life, build strong relationships, and achieve our goals.

Longevity Life

"Ikigai"* means life is to be worthwhile. Ikigai is a purpose that guides you throughout your life and pushes you to make things happen until the moment of your death. The purpose of life is so important in Japanese culture that our idea of retirement simply doesn't exist there, and their longevity five secrets are:

Don’t worry. 2. Cultivate good habits. 3. Nurture your friendships every day. 4. Live an unhurried life. 5. Be optimistic.

Ikigai is different for all of us, but one thing we have in common is that we are all searching for meaning. Our intuition and curiosity are very powerful internal compasses that help us connect with our Ikigai. Happiness is in the doing, not in the result. Life is not a problem to be solved. The sense of community and the fact that Japanese people make an effort to stay retired until the very end are key elements of the secret to a long life. If you want to stay busy even when there is no need to work, there has to be an ikigai on your horizon, a purpose that guides you throughout your life and pushes you to make things of beauty and utility for the community and yourself. If you still have not found your Ikigai, then your mission is to discover it.

The ten rules of Ikigai:

1. Stay active; don't retire.
2. Take it slow.
3. Don’t fill your stomach.
4. Surround yourself with good friends.
5. Get in shape for your next birthday.
6. Smile.
7. Reconnect with nature.
8. Give thanks.

9. Live in the moment.
10. Follow your Ikigai.

*Thanks "Ikigai," written by authors Hector Garcia and Francesc Miralles.

Life is easier and enjoyable

when you design and

simplify your life

at all levels.

3. Signifying Simplification

Simplicity

Simplicity is the concept of living a simple and uncomplicated life with minimal possessions, distractions, and unnecessary complexities. Here are some reasons why simplicity is important:

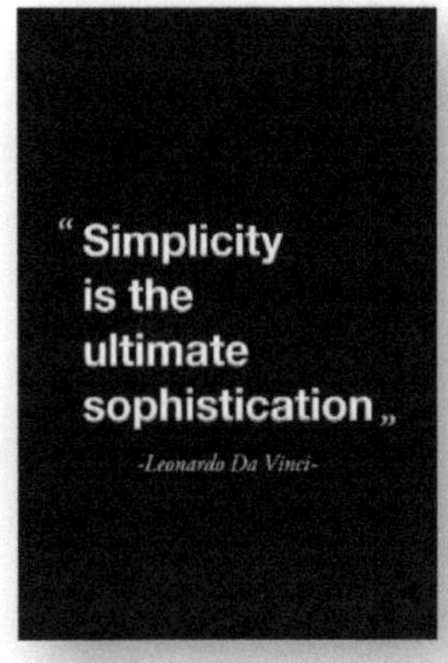

Reduces Stress: A simpler lifestyle can reduce stress and anxiety, as it allows us to focus on what is truly important rather than being overwhelmed by distractions and material possessions.

Encourages Mindfulness: Simplifying our lives can help us be more present and mindful, as we are not distracted by excess possessions and unnecessary activities.

Promotes Financial Freedom: Simplifying our lives can also lead to financial freedom as we reduce our dependence on material possessions and the expenses that come with them.

Reduces Environmental Impact: A simpler lifestyle can also have a positive impact on the environment as it encourages us to reduce waste and conserve resources.

Promotes Health and Well-Being: Living a simpler life can also promote health and well-being, as it

encourages healthy habits such as regular exercise, healthy eating, and stress reduction.

Encourages Creativity: Simplifying our lives can also encourage creativity, as we have more time and mental space to focus on creative pursuits and hobbies.

Simple is not necessarily easy to implement. Simple demands clear vision, and approach with an open mind to take risks. Acceptance of the unacceptable is the greatest source of grace in this world.

Simplification can be applied to a wide range of areas, including:

Time management: Simplifying your schedule and daily routines to reduce stress and increase productivity

Finances: Simplifying your financial life by creating a budget, reducing expenses, and automating bill payments

Relationships: Simplifying your social life by focusing on your closest relationships and reducing obligations that don't align with your values or priorities

Home organization: simplifying your living space by decluttering, minimizing possessions, and creating systems for organization and maintenance

Work processes: Simplifying work processes by reducing unnecessary steps, automating tasks, and focusing on high-priority tasks

Simplification is often associated with minimalism and can be an effective way to reduce stress, increase focus, and improve well-being. By eliminating distractions and focusing on what is most important, individuals can create a more fulfilling and meaningful life.

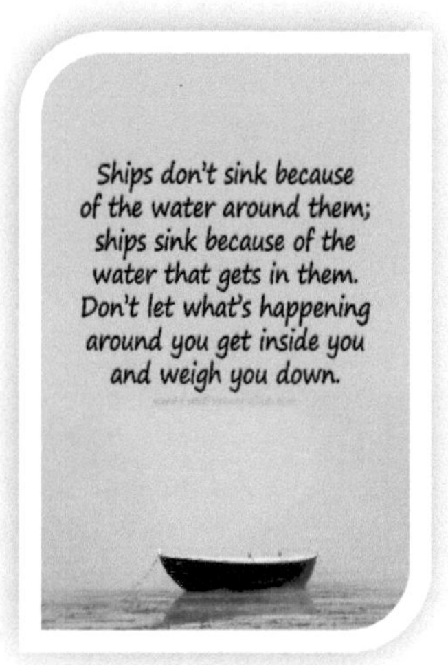

Simple work can resolve an umpteen number of problems, like having a single key for two inmates in a hostel room, which creates a lot of problems because one person has to depend on another roommate for everything, forcing them to waste a lot of time and resulting in unwanted arguments, mistrust, and disagreements. However, a simple task of making one duplicate key can resolve all their unnecessary tension and problems once and for all. Hence, we can manage everything by simplifying everything. The same way our lives are easily manageable and enjoyable if we simplify our lifestyle at all levels,

Simplify everything to ease our lives. Because complicating is easy and simplifying is difficult, we complicate ourselves and try to solve with others. Our day-to-day lives can be eased through the simple simplification of operating procedures, sometimes without any additional financial burden. You can do anything, but not everything. Life is a journey to be experienced, not a problem to be solved.

In conclusion, simplicity is an important concept that can promote stress reduction, mindfulness, financial freedom, environmental responsibility, health and well-being, and creativity. By embracing simplicity and living a more minimalist lifestyle, we can focus on what is truly important in life and live a more fulfilling and meaningful existence. In the context of personal or professional life, simplification often involves reducing complexity, removing unnecessary elements, and focusing on what is most important.

Honesty

Honesty is the quality of being truthful and straightforward in all our interactions with others. It is an important value in personal relationships, work, and society as a whole. Here are some reasons why honesty is important:

Builds Trust: Honesty fosters interpersonal trust. When you are honest with someone, they are more likely to trust you and feel comfortable confiding in you.

Encourages Open Communication: Open communication is essential for developing strong relationships and fostering effective communication. When people are honest with each other, they can communicate more effectively, resolving conflicts and reaching mutually agreeable solutions.

Fosters Accountability: Honesty encourages personal responsibility and accountability. When people are honest about their actions, they take ownership of their behavior, which is an important trait for personal growth and development.

Encourages Honesty: Honesty is essential for fairness and justice. When people are honest, they ensure that others are treated fairly and justly.

Builds Credibility: Honest people are often viewed as more credible, reliable, and trustworthy. This is particularly important in professional settings, where credibility and trust are crucial for success.

Encourages Ethical Behavior: Honesty is an essential component of ethical behavior. People who are honest are more likely to act ethically and with integrity in their personal and professional lives.

Honesty is an important value that promotes trust, communication, accountability, fairness, credibility, and ethical behavior. By practicing honesty in all areas of life, we can build stronger relationships, contribute to a better society, and be better versions of ourselves.

Humility

Humility is the quality of being modest and unassuming, and it is considered an important virtue in many cultures and traditions. Here are some reasons why humility is important:

Encourages open-mindedness: people who are humble are often more open to new ideas and experiences. They do not let their egos get in the way of learning and growth.

Builds Stronger Relationships: Humility can help build stronger, more meaningful relationships. When we approach others with humility, we are less likely to be defensive and more likely to listen and communicate effectively.

Increases Empathy: Humility allows us to see things from others' perspectives, which can increase our empathy and understanding.

Fosters Gratitude: Humility helps us appreciate the contributions of others and the opportunities we have been given, which can lead to greater gratitude and contentment.

Encourages Personal Growth: Humble people are more open to feedback and criticism, which can help them identify areas for personal growth and improvement.

Encourages Service: Humility often leads to a desire to serve others and make a positive impact on the world. Humble people are often motivated by a desire to help others rather than personal gain.

Humility is an important virtue that can promote open-mindedness, empathy, gratitude, personal growth, and service to others. By practicing humility, we can build stronger relationships, contribute to a better society, and be better versions of ourselves.

Morality

Morality refers to a set of principles and values that guide an individual's behavior and decision-making. It is concerned with what is right and wrong, good and bad, and what ought to be done in a given situation. Morality is influenced by various factors such as culture, religion, personal beliefs, and social norms.

At its core, morality is about treating others with respect, empathy, and kindness. It involves considering the consequences of our actions and making choices that promote the well-being of ourselves and others. Moral behavior is often associated with virtues such as honesty, fairness, compassion, and integrity.

However, morality is not always clear-cut, and people can hold different opinions about what is right and wrong. For example, some may believe that it is morally acceptable to tell a lie to protect someone's feelings, while others may believe that honesty should always be prioritized. Such differences can give rise to ethical dilemmas, where there is no obvious right or wrong answer.

Morality is an important aspect of human behavior and plays a crucial role in how we interact with others and make decisions. While there may be disagreements about specific moral issues, a commitment to treating others with respect and consideration is essential to maintaining a just and compassionate society.

Living with Harmony

Living without any animosity is possible, although it may be challenging for some people. Animosities are negative emotions or feelings that arise when we experience conflict, resentment, or hostility towards others. These feelings can cause stress, anxiety, and tension in our relationships and can impact our physical and mental health.

However, by practicing empathy, compassion, and forgiveness, we can reduce the animosity that we feel towards others and create a more positive and harmonious environment. Here are some ways to live without any animosity:

Practice Empathy: By putting ourselves in the shoes of others and trying to understand their perspectives and experiences, we can develop a greater sense of compassion and empathy towards them. This can help us overcome negative feelings and attitudes towards others.

Cultivate Forgiveness: Forgiveness can be a powerful tool for reducing animosity and resentment towards others. By forgiving those who have hurt us, we can release negative emotions and move towards a more positive and peaceful relationship.

Focus on Common Ground: By focusing on common ground and shared values with others, we can reduce feelings of animosity and create a more collaborative and cooperative environment.

Communicate Effectively: By practicing effective communication, we can reduce misunderstandings, conflicts, and negative feelings towards others. Listening actively, expressing our needs and emotions clearly, and seeking to understand others' perspectives can create a more positive and respectful relationship.

In conclusion, while it may be challenging, it is possible to live without any animosity by practicing empathy, forgiveness, focusing on common ground, and communicating effectively. These practices can help us create more positive and harmonious relationships with others and reduce negative emotions and feelings in our lives.

Harmony of My Father's Life

"Simple life" is nothing, as my father's life and his life journey relied on simplicity, honesty, humility, and morality. He gave us full freedom and allowed us to handle our responsibilities by ourselves to keep up our individuality. He never forced anything on others and only wished not to hurt or harm anyone in any way. We respected the freedom given by my parents, and the entrusted responsibilities made us use it judiciously.

He was free from materialistic high-value products, including high-value gold, money, or any property. He never had any personal place to store anything except one small drawer, which contained old letters, old communication documents, and old passports but not gold

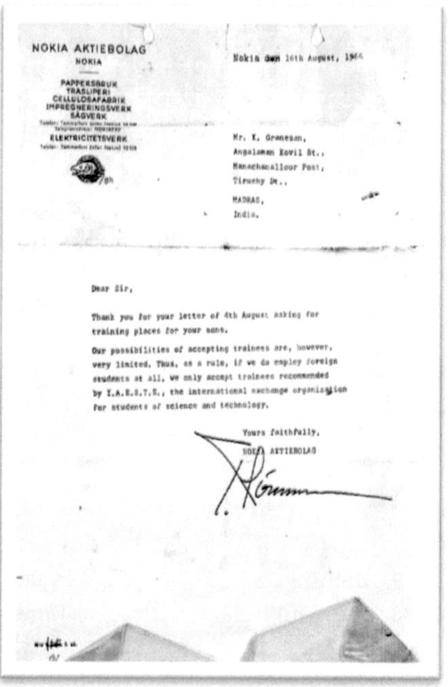
NOKIA AKTIEBOLAG
NOKIA

PAPPERSBRUK
TRÄSLIPERI
CELLULOSAFABRIK
IMPREGNERINGSVERK
SÅGVERK

ELEKTRICITETSVERK

Nokia den 16th August, 196[illegible]

Mr. K. Ganesan,
Angalaman Kovil St.,
Manachanallour Post,
Tiruchy Dt.,
MADRAS,
India.

Dear Sir,

Thank you for your letter of 4th August asking for training places for your sons.

Our possibilities of accepting trainees are, however, very limited. Thus, as a rule, if we do employ foreign students at all, we only accept trainees recommended by I.A.E.S.T.E., the international exchange organization for students of science and technology.

Yours faithfully,
NOKIA AKTIEBOLAG

or money. He never had any personal gold items or liked to wear gold in any form, expect for a leather strap watch he used on a few occasions.

All he owned and loved were a few khadi shirts, dhotis, towels, an Indian Railway timetable, and Hindu newspapers. He was interested in writing letters to explore places all over the world (he even received responses from Nokia Owner Mr. Nokia, India's President office,

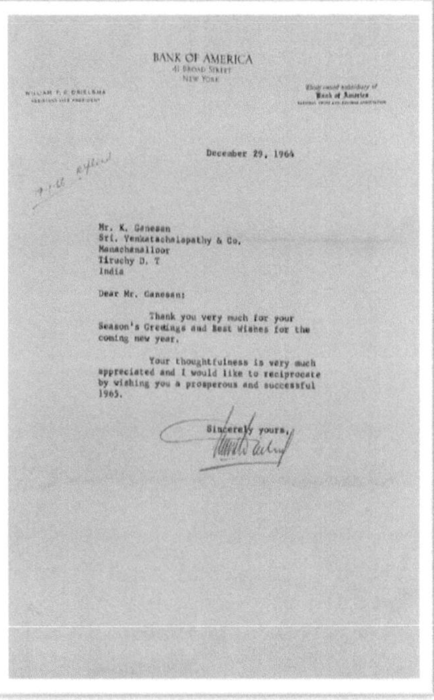

BANK OF AMERICA
41 Broad Street
New York

December 29, 1964

Mr. K. Ganesan
Sri. Venkatachalapathy & Co.
Manachanalloor
Tiruchy D. T
India

Dear Mr. Ganesan:

Thank you very much for your Season's Greetings and Best Wishes for the coming new year.

Your thoughtfulness is very much appreciated and I would like to reciprocate by wishing you a prosperous and successful 1965.

Sincerely yours,

Chairman, Bank of America, and even the owner of Play Boy, etc.), reading all classified columns, letters to the editor, and playing cricket (St. Anthony's College, Kandy

Cricket team member in the 1930s).The Lord Ganesh temple in Andapuram, Namakkal district, Tamil Nadu, India, was constructed and consecrated in the 1920s by my grandfather to fulfil an earnest wish of my father's birth and, later in 1923, was named Ganesan for my father.

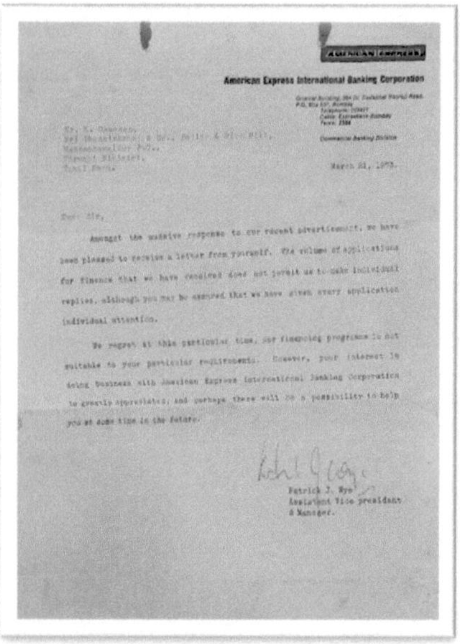

AMERICAN EXPRESS

American Express International Banking Corporation

Commercial Banking Division

Dear Sir,

Amongst the massive response to our recent advertisement, we have been pleased to receive a letter from yourself. The volume of applications for finance that we have received does not permit us to make individual replies, although you may be assured that we have given every application individual attention.

We regret at this particular time, our financing programme is not suitable to your particular requirements. However, your interest in doing business with American Express International Banking Corporation is greatly appreciated, and perhaps there will be a possibility to help you at some time in the future.

Patrick J. Nye
Assistant Vice president
& Manager.

He loved travelling and used to travel anywhere for any number of days with one yellow bag (Manja Pai), which would have one ordinary towel and a pocket knife (to cut fruits). He used to wear a white khadi cotton shirt in which the pocket carried an ink pen, a tiny diary (having contact details), and some money, but not in a money purse.

The following are three incidents that speak to my father's humility, honesty, and morality:

Humility: He had a high level of humility and never had any animosity with anyone in his life. Throughout his life, he harbored no hatred for anyone or anything and never fostered animosity. He used to narrate things in a way that the recipient could understand in a very simplified way to make others comfortable. One day, my mother and I overheard my father's narrative about us to a distant relative regarding our jobs in a simple way, like "the eldest son is telling that he is doing some business, like rice bran, the next one is working in a boiler company, the

next one is working in a truck company, and the last one, being the youngest, is saying that he is studying in an institute." The man who listened was very happy and was of the opinion that his sons were better placed than others.

"No need to worry, the man who works in the boiler can own a shop later and make tea as he has experience with the boiler (in reality, he was an engineer at BHEL, taking care of boilers), the next one will slowly own a truck from cleaner status, and the last one is good to learn and join as a typist." The reality was that the first one was a whole sale rice merchant, the second one was working for BHEL, the third one was working for Ashok Leyland, and I was studying post-graduation at a premier institute.

Honesty: Once, a bus owner came from a long distance to my home to get blessings from my father because the owner was astonished to receive a small amount through a money order. The incident was that my father went on his usual pilgrimage trip to Vaitheeswaran Temple, near

Kumbakonam, Tamil Nadu, India. Due to overcrowding,

he was unable to purchase a bus ticket from Sirkazhi to Vaitheeswaran Temple because of the heavy crowd.

However, he noted down the private bus company name, found other details for ticket payment, and sent money through a money order to the owner of the bus company. The simplicity and honesty of my father made the bus owner very happy, and he came all the way down to get my father's blessing.

Morality: When I was ten years old, I found a pair of abandoned slippers on the riverbed and were perfectly fitting for me, and others told me to wear them and go home. My mother was talking about the slippers when we all sat down for lunch, and my father got annoyed and told

me to go immediately and leave the slippers where you

have picked them up. My mother was telling me at the time to let him finish his lunch and then he would leave the slippers at home. My father, on the other hand, insisted that I return the slippers to where I had picked them up before I ate lunch. This was the sole purpose—not to make the other person suffer for his lost items. I was about to touch the food but got up and walked down to the river to leave slippers at the same place. This small incident taught me the value of proper upbringing. I have tried to adopt his ideals and morality in my day-to-day life.

"Do not handicap

your children

by making their

lives easy".

Robert A Heinlein

4. Educating and Parenting

Education is the process of acquiring knowledge, skills, values, beliefs, and habits through various forms of learning, including formal education, informal education, and experiential learning. Education is critical in the development of individuals, communities, and societies, as it equips individuals with the tools they need to succeed in life and contribute to the progress of their communities.

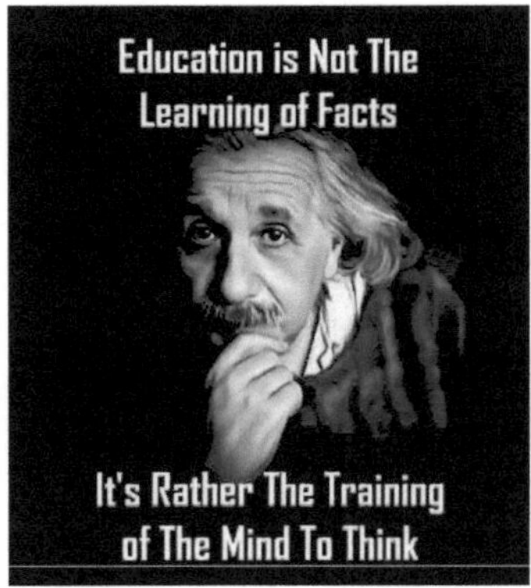

Education is essential for personal growth and development. It enables individuals to acquire knowledge and skills that are necessary for their personal and professional lives. Education helps individuals to become more critical thinkers, better communicators, and problem-solvers. It also promotes creativity, innovation, and entrepreneurship, which are crucial for economic growth and development.

Education also plays a crucial role in social and cultural development. It enables individuals to understand and appreciate their cultural heritage and diversity, and it promotes respect for others' beliefs and values. Education also helps to reduce social inequality by providing equal opportunities for all individuals, regardless of their social and economic backgrounds.

In addition to personal and social development, education is essential for economic development. It provides individuals with the skills and knowledge necessary to engage in productive economic activities, create wealth, and contribute to the development of their communities. Education also promotes technological advancements and scientific research, which are critical for economic growth and development.

There are various forms of education, including formal education, informal education, and experiential learning. Formal education refers to structured learning that takes place in schools, colleges, and universities. Informal education refers to learning that takes place outside formal education settings, such as through reading, social interactions, and practical experiences. Experiential learning involves learning through direct experience and reflection, such as internships, apprenticeships, and service-learning.

Focus of Our Education

Good communications. Mother tongue communication and global communication language

Logical thinking, reasoning, and analysis moral and social values and responsibilities.

The study of culture, hospitality, personal hygiene, and health; yoga and meditation; wellness and social responsibilities; public behavior; and road and transportation safety

Understanding global warming and safeguarding all kinds of natural resources at all levels

Basic sciences of global geography, environment, resources, rivers, animals, trees, and nature

Kids should be taught things like harmonious coexistence—how to live harmoniously and not to hurt or hate anyone. Basic hygiene and how to behave in public, how to use public properties, and how to safeguard public properties and natural resources

Fire safety, road safety, tolerance, compassion, basic health and hygiene, understanding biological phenomena, and coping with and molding psychological behavior to be taught how to simplify the given task. Lessons should focus on creativity and bring out new dimensions. Books should not force their opinion; rather, they should generate new perspectives on the subject. Now we learn most of the time what X, Y, and Z are told about something, but we fail to know about aspiring individuals' fresh thoughts. Experts' opinions are welcome, but at the same time, out of their domain, laymen's points of view will give an unexpected new perspective to the subject. Because a layman's point of view will be different and fresh,

Education starts with the soul and body of an individual and then extends to other subjects along with self-discipline and a healthy lifestyle, and to respecting a fellow human being as well as all living things.

Brain Development

Brain development refers to the process by which the brain grows and matures from birth to childhood and adolescence, and then continues to change throughout

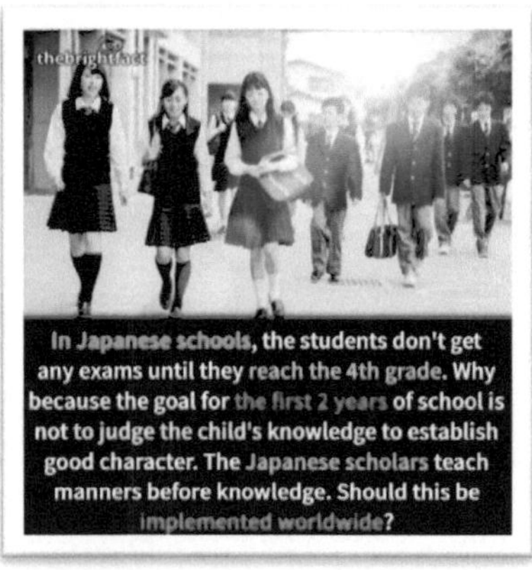

adulthood. It involves the formation of neural connections, the growth and pruning of neural pathways, and the acquisition of new skills and abilities.

Basic subject knowledge is to be taught until the school level. Following the college level of study, students should concentrate on their individual knowledge and thought processes and an individual's point of view on the subject, whose faculty will monitor and develop his or her abilities into useful productivity for the world. College should not force students to learn; instead, students should analyze and speak out from their own perspectives.

Here are some important factors that can affect brain development:

Genetics: Genes play a key role in brain development, influencing the formation of neural connections and the expression of specific brain functions.

Environment: Environmental factors such as nutrition, exposure to toxins, stress, and early life experiences can all impact brain development. Providing a safe, nurturing, and stimulating environment can help support healthy brain development.

Early experiences: The first few years of life are critical for brain development, with experiences during this period shaping the brain's architecture and establishing neural pathways that can have lasting effects on cognitive, social, and emotional development.

Learning and stimulation: learning new skills and engaging in stimulating activities can help promote the growth and development of neural pathways, supporting cognitive and social-emotional development.

Physical activity: Regular physical activity has been shown to support brain development by improving cognitive function and supporting the growth of neural pathways.

In conclusion, brain development is a complex process that is influenced by a variety of factors, including genetics, environment, early experiences, learning, and physical activity. Providing a safe, nurturing, and stimulating environment and engaging in activities that promote learning and physical activity can help support healthy brain development.

School of Thought

The school of thought should encourage creativity, bring out new dimensions in the subject, and teach how to simplify the given task. We now spend most of our time focusing on the creations of others, and we are unaware of our own contribution and creation. Expert theory is well known, but a layman's perspective from outside the domain will add an unexpected valuable dimension to the subject.

Parental care should be like friend care, and teacher care should be like guiding care.

0 to 5 years Health and Basic Knowledge

50% of parents and 50% of teachers engage in social behavior.

6 to 12 years of age Health and Hygiene, Moral Values, Language and Sports and Debate

12 to 18 years old on a weekly basis Parents and teachers should listen to their views and desires.

The six years of observation of their vision and desires should be recorded and monitored periodically to note any unexpected variation at any level. Listening to their voices for a minimum of five minutes on a weekly basis and also asking them to write one page per week of their views and desires on their own in the exclusive Desire Note Diary. A single page per week takes 52 pages in one year. As a result, at the age of 18, their thoughts and desires for the previous six years will fill 6 * 52 = 312 pages. The desired life style design will be framed to fulfil their desires with parents and life style consultants based on 312 pages of their own views and desires from the age of 12 to 18 years.

Life-style consultant role:

12 to 18 years: Desired education and directions

19 to 22 years: Desired career path

23 to 30 years: Life partner, lifestyle, health, and wealth management are all desirable positioning's.

31 to 40 years: Desired objectives like housing, relationships, and offspring well-being are fulfilled.

41 to 50 years: Desired family relationships, social relationships, and retirement progress

51 to 60 years: Wealth and health goals, lifestyle changes, and retirement

61 and above: Desired desire program: health, wealth, soul, and holistic life management

Key Benefits of Education

Here are some of the key benefits of education:

Personal development: Education helps individuals develop critical thinking skills, creativity, and a lifelong love of learning, which can lead to personal growth and development.

Career opportunities: Education can provide individuals with the skills and qualifications necessary to pursue a wide range of career opportunities and improve their earning potential.

Social and cultural awareness: Education can promote social and cultural awareness, tolerance, and understanding, which can lead to a more peaceful and harmonious society.

Better health and well-being: Education can promote healthy behavior's and lifestyles, leading to better health outcomes and an overall better quality of life.

Economic development: Education can contribute to economic development. Personal empowerment: Education can empower individuals to take control of their lives and make informed decisions, improving their well-being and that of their families and communities.

In conclusion, education is a fundamental human right that plays a crucial role in personal, social, and economic development. It provides individuals with the knowledge, skills, values, and attitudes necessary to pursue fulfilling careers, contribute to society, and lead fulfilling lives. Overall, education is an essential tool for survival and success in life, as it provides individuals with the knowledge and skills necessary to navigate the world and achieve their goals.

Dos and Don'ts for Teachers

Dos:

- Create a positive and inclusive classroom environment. Make sure that all students feel welcome and valued in your classroom.
- Build relationships with your students. Getting to know your students on a personal level can help you better understand their needs and interests.
- Use a variety of teaching methods—a combination of visual, auditory, and hands-on learning activities—to cater to different learning styles.

- Encourage student engagement: encourage your students to ask questions, participate in discussions, and take an active role in their own learning.
- Provide timely and constructive feedback. Give your students timely feedback on their work, and be sure to provide constructive criticism that helps them improve.
- Keep up-to-date with current educational trends and research. Continue to learn and grow as a teacher by staying informed on the latest developments in education.
- Communicate effectively with parents; keep them informed about their child's progress and any concerns you may have.
- Collaborate with colleagues. Work with other teachers to share ideas and resources and to develop a more cohesive educational program.
- Encourage critical thinking. Help your students develop critical thinking skills by asking open-ended questions and encouraging them to analyze and evaluate information.
- Model positive behavior's and attitudes; set a positive example for your students by modelling respect, kindness, and a love of learning.

Don'ts:

- Don't show favoritism; treat all students fairly and avoid showing preference for any particular student.

- Don't be overly critical; avoid criticizing students in a way that damages their self-esteem or discourages them from learning.
- Don't use sarcasm or humor that belittles students; be mindful of your tone and avoid using humor that may be perceived as hurtful.
- Don't let your own biases or prejudices affect your teaching; be aware of your own biases and work to overcome them.
- Don't give too much homework; be mindful of your students' workload outside of the classroom and avoid giving too much homework.
- Don't ignore signs of struggling students; be attuned to signs that a student may be struggling and provide support and resources to help them succeed.
- Don't be dismissive of student concerns; take student concerns seriously and work to address any issues that arise.
- Don't teach to the test; prioritize learning and growth over test scores.
- Don't be afraid to ask for help; seek guidance and support from colleagues, administrators, and other educational professionals when needed.
- Don't give up on struggling students; persist in finding ways to help them and provide them with the resources and support they need to succeed.

Parenting

Parenting is the process of raising and nurturing children from infancy to adulthood. Effective parenting involves providing love, guidance, and support to help children grow and develop into responsible and well-adjusted adults.

It's important for parents to communicate with their children in a respectful and empathetic manner, treating

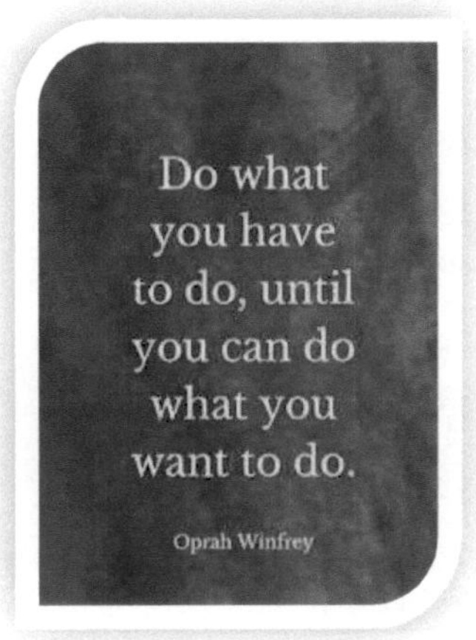

them as individuals with their own thoughts, feelings, and perspectives. This involves listening actively, speaking honestly and openly, and acknowledging their child's thoughts and feelings.

Effective parenting involves providing love, guidance, and support to help children grow and develop into responsible and well-adjusted adults. It's a challenging and rewarding responsibility that requires patience, consistency, and a willingness to learn and adapt

Remember, every child is different, and what works for one child may not work for another. It's important to be flexible, patient, and understanding as you navigate the journey of raising a child.

Most of the problems in life are because of two reasons: we act without thinking or we keep thinking without acting.

Patronizing, on the other hand, refers to an attitude or behavior in which a person speaks or behaves in a condescending or superior manner towards another person. It involves treating someone as if they are inferior or incapable of understanding or doing something.

While parenting involves providing guidance and support to children, patronizing them can be harmful and disrespectful. It can make the other person feel belittled, disrespected, or powerless, which can damage relationships.

Do not impose the "Tree Pattern" life cycle on your kids to get the same results like seed, flower, and fruit form. Do not expect your child to give you what you want. In that way, animals are better at handling their offspring because they guard them for a short period of time, then they themselves explore the world and do everything according to their preferences.

The ability to observe without judgement is the highest form of intelligence. Parents are not sworn to control or monitor their children at all times. Freedom makes people stronger because it allows them to learn good and bad things. In general, parents wanted the best scenario all the time, like success, top grades, top positions, etc., but eventually missed the reality of facing the other side of the worst scenario.

Parenting is not about acting like a cop, but it is our responsibility to ensure that kids are comfortable enough to freely exchange their views, likes, and dislikes. Spare the rod, raise the child through effective communication in accordance with their level of mind.

Spare the Rod, Raise the Child

I used the same method for my son's upbringing. Whenever he did not listen or disobey, I would compare him to a buffalo and explain that a buffalo would not listen or obey unless someone beats it with a rod. However, humans should not harm or beat any animal, including buffaloes, as they are social animals who live in natural harmony. Then, I would remind him that I considered him an intelligent boy who could understand and follow our advice. However, if he did not, unfortunately, he would become like a buffalo, and everyone would metaphorically "beat" him. Whenever he did something wrong, I would ask him a question, "Are you a buffalo or a good boy?" He would immediately respond, "I am not a buffalo; I am a good boy, and I will do it correctly." Gradually, over the years, my son's attitude towards his studies and respect for others changed significantly. The blessings of our parents motivated him to do well in life.

At the age of two, my son was drawn to the Compaq Presario desktop computer, and I allowed him to use it without supervision, explaining the do's and don'ts, such as not touching electrical sockets or the back portion of the computer panel. He learned many things on his own through the trial-and-error method and became computer-savvy at an early age. A free mind fosters creativity and allows one to excel in all aspects, whereas a controlled mind is rigid and fails to excel. Therefore, we should allow our children to think freely, with only limited restrictions, in order to explore their imagination, allowing for infinite possibilities.

In conclusion, while parenting and patronizing are two different concepts, effective parenting involves communicating with children in a respectful and empathetic manner, while patronizing involves treating someone as inferior or incapable. It's important to be aware of these differences and strive to communicate with others in a way that is respectful and supportive.

Dos and Don'ts for Parents

Dos and don'ts for parents while bringing up their children:

Dos:

- Spend quality time with your children; this means engaging with them, listening to them, and being present in their lives.
- Provide a nurturing and supportive environment. Children thrive in an environment that is safe, loving, and supportive.
- Set clear and consistent boundaries. Children need structure and consistency in order to feel safe and secure.

- Encourage open communication. Foster a positive and open environment where your children feel comfortable sharing their thoughts and feelings.
- Be a positive role model. Children often learn through observation, so it's important to model positive behaviors and attitudes.
- Encourage your child's independence. As your child grows older, it's important to encourage them to become more independent and self-reliant.
- Foster a love of learning by encouraging your child's curiosity and providing opportunities for them to explore new interests.
- Teach empathy and kindness. Help your child understand the value of empathy and kindness towards others. Support your child's emotional and mental health. Celebrate your child's accomplishments. Take time to acknowledge and celebrate your child's achievements and successes.

Don'ts:

- Don't use physical punishment; physical punishment can be harmful to a child's mental and emotional well-being.
- Don't be overprotective; it's important to allow your child to experience age-appropriate challenges and take calculated risks.
- Don't compare your child to others; every child is unique, and comparing them to others can be damaging to their self-esteem.
- Don't use negative reinforcement; instead of punishing negative behaviors, focus on reinforcing positive behaviors.
- Don't ignore your child's emotions; it's important to be attuned to your child's emotions and to provide them with support and understanding.
- Don't pressure your child to perform; instead of focusing solely on achievements and outcomes, prioritize the process and effort involved in the learning process.

- Don't neglect your child's physical health; make sure your child gets enough sleep, exercise, and healthy food.
- Don't dismiss your child's interests; even if their interests don't align with your own, it's important to support and encourage their passions.
- Don't be inconsistent with rules and consequences; children need consistency in order to feel safe and secure.
- Don't priorities your own needs over your child's; as a parent, it's important to put your child's needs first and to be attentive to their well-being.

“Money should always

be kept in circulation.

If you horde it for a rainy day,

you will have to spend it on an ark”.

5. Caring Health and Wealth

Health and wealth are two important aspects of our lives that are interconnected in various ways. While wealth can provide resources to maintain good health, good health is also essential for creating and maintaining wealth.

Health and wealth are interconnected in various ways, and investing in one can have positive impacts on the other. By prioritizing both health and wealth, individuals can create a more fulfilling and financially stable life.

Here are some ways in which health and wealth are interconnected:

Financial stability: Good health can help individuals maintain financial stability. Poor health can lead to increased medical bills and missed work, which can impact an individual's earning potential and financial stability.

Increased productivity: Good health can lead to increased productivity and better performance at work. This can lead to higher earnings and more opportunities for career advancement.

Long-term savings: Investing in good health can lead to long-term savings. For example, by engaging in healthy behaviors such as regular exercise and healthy eating, individuals can reduce their risk of chronic illnesses and save money on medical bills in the long run.

Better quality of life: Good health can improve an individual's quality of life and overall well-being, which can lead to a greater sense of happiness and satisfaction.

Access to resources: Wealth can provide individuals with access to resources that promote good health, such as high-quality healthcare, healthy food options, and opportunities for physical activity.

Health

Health can be defined as a state of physical, mental, and social well-being. It is a complex concept that

encompasses a wide range of factors, including genetics, lifestyle choices, environmental factors, and access to healthcare.

Maintaining good health is crucial for leading a fulfilling and productive life. It allows individuals to pursue their goals, engage in meaningful relationships, and participate fully in their communities. Good health also provides a sense of vitality and energy, which can improve overall quality of life.

There are many different factors that contribute to good health. Some of these include maintaining a balanced diet, getting regular exercise, managing stress levels, getting adequate sleep, and avoiding harmful substances such as tobacco and drugs. Additionally, access to quality healthcare is important for preventing and treating illnesses and injuries. It is important to recognize that health is not a static state, but rather a dynamic process that requires ongoing attention and care. By making healthy choices and seeking appropriate medical care, individuals can maintain and improve their health over time.

Ultimately, good health is essential for living a happy and fulfilling life, and should be prioritized and valued accordingly.

Health refers to a state of physical, mental, and social well-being. It is not just the absence of illness or disease but also the presence of positive factors that contribute to overall well-being. Some important factors that contribute to good health include:

A healthy diet: Eating a balanced diet that is rich in nutrients can help maintain physical health and support mental well-being.

Regular exercise: Engaging in regular physical activity can help maintain physical fitness, reduce the risk of chronic diseases, and improve mental health.

Adequate sleep: Getting enough sleep is crucial for physical and mental health, as it allows the body to repair and rejuvenate itself.

Managing stress: High levels of stress can negatively impact both physical and mental health. It is important to develop coping strategies, such as meditation, exercise, or counselling, to manage stress.

Positive relationships: Cultivating positive relationships with family, friends, and community members can provide a sense of connection and support that contributes to overall well-being.

Preventive care: Regular check-ups, screenings, and other preventive care measures can help identify potential health issues early on and prevent the development of serious health problems.

By prioritizing these factors and taking a holistic approach to health, individuals can work towards achieving optimal physical, mental, and social well-being.

Mental Health

Mental health is an essential aspect of overall health and well-being. It refers to a person's emotional, psychological, and social well-being and can impact the way they think, feel, and behave.

Maintaining good mental health is important because it can affect many areas of life, including personal relationships, work productivity, and physical health. Good mental health can also improve resilience to stress and support the ability to cope with life's challenges.

Conversely, poor mental health can negatively affect all aspects of life, leading to a range of problems including mood disorders, anxiety, and substance abuse. It is important to prioritize mental health in order to prevent or manage these issues.

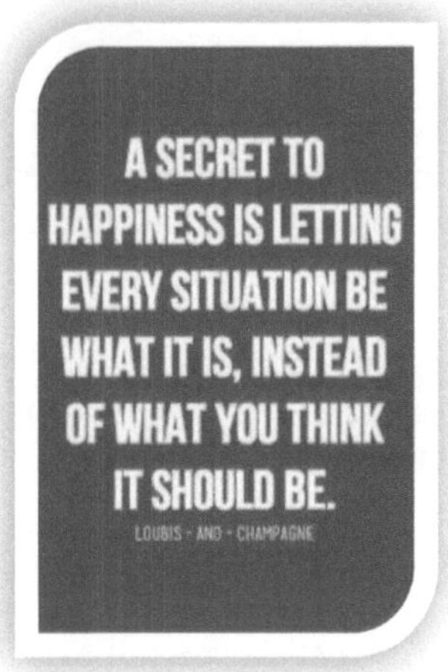

Taking care of mental health involves practices such as developing healthy coping mechanisms, engaging in regular exercise, getting enough sleep, and seeking support when needed. It can also involve accessing professional mental health services, such as therapy or counselling, to help address mental health concerns.

Overall, recognizing the importance of mental health and taking steps to prioritize it can lead to greater well-being and quality of life.

Social Health

Health is not an individual issue or concern, but it is an issue or concern for everyone on the planet. Taking care of one's health is a mandatory and primary duty of any individual; otherwise, their presence burdens the entire world. Hence, caring for your health is not only for you but for the betterment of your entire family, your society, your area, town, city, country, and the world. If you don't take care of your body, then who is going to?

IT'S NOT A
SHORT TERM
DIET. IT'S A
LONG TERM
LIFESTYLE CHANGE.

We should consider "invited sickness" like sickness from smoking, consumption of alcohol, drugs, and immoral activities as a punishable offense. Moreover, obesity could be considered an "invited sickness" for certain categories of people. Invited sick people burden the family, company, hospital resources, insurance companies, and concerned governments' exchequers. Hence, caring for your health is nothing but caring for your country.

Educationalists should give a minimum of 25% weight to health as an integral part of their academic grading's. All types of incentives, rebates, or concessions from the government or corporations need to be stopped for "invited sickness" people, till they achieve their basic health parameters. However, current practice gives rewards for those who are not taking care of their health in many ways, like treatment, medicine, insurance, leave, etc. All public servants, like members of parliament, members of assemblies' legislatures, corporations, municipalities, and village local bodies, must fulfil the prescribed medical fitness requirements to be in public service.

We used to value and give high priority and attention to objects that were trivial in our lives but failed to give importance to maintaining the health of our own invaluable soul and body for an hour, which has thousands of parts and works 365 days a year on a 24*7 basis to keep you alive without using any spare parts.

"Don't just have career or academic goals. Set goals to give you a balanced, successful life. Balanced means ensuring your health, relationship, and mental peace are all in good order. "There is no point in getting a promotion on the day of your breakup." Quote on health: Rattan N. Tata

Health does not always come from medicine. Our food should be our medicine. Most of the time, it comes from peace of mind, peace of the heart, and peace of the soul. It comes from laughter and love. The six best doctors are:

sunshine, water, rest, air, exercise, and diet. Health is not a short-term diet. It's a long-term lifestyle change.

Wealth

"Wealth is the ability to fully experience life" (Henry David Thoreau).

We have traditionally been trained and taught to save money, but we have failed to learn how to use our saved money wisely. The continuous cycle of earning and saving money can become unstoppable until we reach a point of deteriorating health, at which point we spend all our earnings to restore our health. Money is supposed to make our lives more comfortable and enjoyable, but our obsession with it can make our lives demanding and miserable. Even when we reach the age of 70 and beyond, we are still worried about our future and fail to live comfortably in the present or future. It is like the "betel leaf" story, where a person always used the old leaf instead of the fresh one, thinking that the fresh one would go to waste the next day. But he failed to realize that he was never able to enjoy the fresh leaf. 'Wealth is a mindset.'

When we store money for our siblings like animal fodder in the name of the future, we fail to understand the uniqueness of being human and to allow them to earn and lead their lives according to their own desires. If we store enough money to feed our siblings for their future purposes, then we are not bringing up humans; it is nothing but equating them with animals. The best way to live is the Japanese "ukiyo-e" way of living, which means living in the moment. 'Richness is not about what you have; it is about who you are'—Bob Pontoon."

Wealth can be defined as the abundance of valuable resources, including money, assets, and material possessions. While wealth is often associated with financial success and material prosperity, it can also refer to other forms of abundance, such as knowledge, relationships, and health.

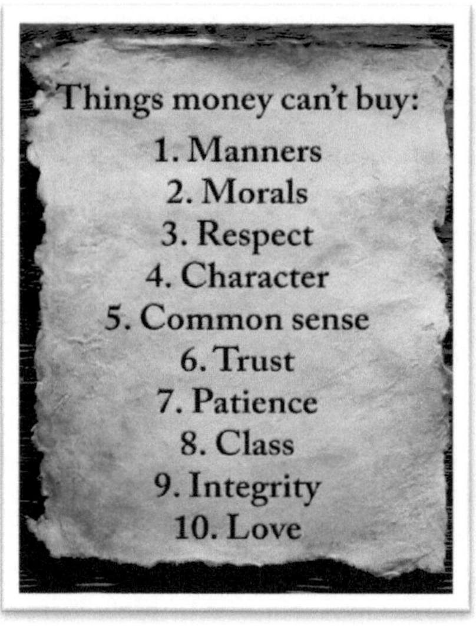

The pursuit of wealth is a common goal for many individuals, as it can provide financial security, social status, and a sense of accomplishment. However, the accumulation of wealth can also come with its own set of challenges, such as managing finances, balancing work and personal life, and navigating social expectations.

It is important to note that wealth is not a guarantee of happiness or fulfillment. While financial stability can certainly improve one's quality of life, studies have shown that there is a limit to the correlation between wealth and happiness. In fact, excessive wealth can lead to its own set of problems, such as isolation, mistrust, and a lack of purpose.

Ultimately, the pursuit of wealth should be balanced with other values, such as personal growth, meaningful relationships, and social responsibility. By seeking a well-rounded approach to life, we can create a sense of wealth that goes beyond material possessions and reflects our deeper values and aspirations.

While wealth is often associated with money, it is important to note that it encompasses more than just financial resources. Wealth can include a range of valuable assets, such as property, investments, and possessions, as well as non-financial resources such as education, health, relationships, and experiences.

Furthermore, the concept of wealth is subjective and can vary depending on an individual's perspective and values. For some, wealth may mean having a large amount of money or material possessions, while for others, it may mean having a fulfilling career, a strong social support network, or the ability to pursue one's passions and interests.

Ultimately, wealth is a complex and multifaceted concept that cannot be reduced solely to financial resources. It encompasses a range of assets and resources that contribute to an individual's overall well-being and quality of life.

Money Matters

Money is the most trusted material to test human nature. Money, they argue, whether for good or evil, is part of human nature. Human behavior towards money can't be solely explained by its utility; it has a more addictive quality—like a drug. According to Professors Lea and Webley, money is more than just a tool for us; it also acts as a drug on the mind. Drugs act on the central nervous

system to create mental states that do not fulfil some kind

of function in the world in the same way that sex or food do. For example, the feeling of hunger drives us to find food, and we need food to survive, so hunger has an evolutionary function. Part of the attraction of money, however, like drugs, is that it changes how we feel, but this change has no biological or evolutionary significance. Part of the benefit people derive from acquiring money—e.g., making us feel good—does not lead to some actual benefit in the world; it is just chasing money for the sake of having money.

Compared to other animals, humans take a long time to grow up, and while growing up and still afterwards, we have a strong instinct for play. Perhaps our inclination for play naturally provides part of the platform on which we have built our addiction to money. Money turns out to be one of the most addictive games we've ever invented. Money is more than just a useful tool, as some economists have argued; while money is certainly useful, human behavior towards it can't be explained just by its utility. The drug metaphor helps demonstrate how the motivation for money often extends past its actual utility. This ties in with many sociological analyses that emphasize money's social meaning and symbolic nature over and above its simple utilitarian applications.

To balance your current lifestyle with your retirement goals, start by assessing your current situation and setting new lifestyle goals. Then create a plan to achieve those goals within your budget and monitor your progress over time.

In order to assess your financial situation, ask yourself questions about how happy your current lifestyle makes you and how you're handling your money. Develop a new lifestyle and retirement goals if your current ones are incompatible. Design a strategy for ensuring our goals can coexist, and be sure to check and update your plan every three months.

If you find a disconnect between your lifestyle goals and your retirement goals, it very likely means you need to either develop new goals or revise your existing ones. Make sure that these goals are realistic based on your financial resources. Again, you will need to distinguish your wants from your needs. "Wealth isn't having a lot of money; it's having a lot of options," says Chris Rock.

To help you stay on track with your lifestyle goals, make a written list of the things you want to do—a list of things that could make your life more pleasurable. This "pleasure list" can include, but is not limited to, hobbies you'd like to pursue, places you'd like to go, restaurants you want to try, places where you want to live, the kind of car you want to drive, and charities you'd like to support.

Travel and Ease

Travel and ease refers to the idea of making travel as stress-free and enjoyable as possible. It involves planning ahead, packing efficiently, and being mindful of one's own needs and limitations. By taking steps to minimize the stress of travel, we can more fully enjoy the experience of exploring new places.

Travel isn't just about getting to your destination. Travel begins the moment you consider it, pack your belongings, and leave your house. Travel or a journey starts at home and ends when you return home. A good trip is not one that has been meticulously planned and meticulously scheduled. Travel takes its own path as it moves from one point to another, taking any bend, curve, or turn along the way. Travel requires planning ahead of time with a flexible schedule and comforts, but it should never be rigid. If it is point-to-point, then it may be considered an official trip. You are your own travel guide because you

are a human being, and you may like certain things that others would have ignored to mention.

Simplify your travel to enjoy maximum flexibility in all levels of materialistic comfort like food, mode of transport, hotel facilities, etc. As you're going to the moon, don't bring too many items. Travel with an open mind to adopt or change anything on your journey, like missing flights, which could be enjoyable and experienced at airports.

Travel as you wish and choose a place to reach leisurely. Walk around and engage people over there, and enjoy everything like their culture, food, dance, etc. Travel like a local and get the best feel of the country. However, many of us take a flight and reach a hotel, then reach all the tourist destinations by car and take a few photos to complete all formalities like "Tourist Jobs or Duties." It is

not a job to do; it is a joyous and pleasant experience.

There are many ways to incorporate travel and ease into your next trip. Some tips include: researching your destination ahead of time, packing light and bringing only essentials, organizing your travel documents and itinerary, and taking breaks to rest and recharge when needed. Ultimately, the goal of travel and ease is to allow travelers to fully immerse themselves in the experience of travel, without the distractions and stressors that can detract from the journey. By embracing this concept, we can make the most of our travels and create memories that will last a lifetime. Travel refers to the act of moving from one place to another for the purpose of recreation, exploration, business, or any other reason. It typically involves transportation, such as by car, plane, train, or boat, and may also involve overnight stays in hotels or other accommodations. Travel can be domestic or international, and may involve short trips, weekend getaways, or extended stays in foreign countries. It is a way for individuals to experience new cultures, meet new people, and broaden their perspectives on the world.

Present-day travel has become an essential part of human life, allowing people to explore new places, learn about different cultures, and broaden their horizons. Traveling is no longer a luxury reserved for the wealthy; rather, it has become more accessible and affordable, thanks to advancements in transportation, technology, and tourism infrastructure.

LIFE IS
TOO SHORT
TO BE
UNHAPPY

Traveling provides numerous benefits for humans, both individually and as a society. It can help reduce stress, improve mental health, and foster personal growth and self-discovery. It also provides opportunities for cultural exchange, creating a more diverse and tolerant world. Additionally, travel can stimulate economic growth by creating jobs and generating revenue for local businesses.

In the wake of the COVID-19 pandemic, travel has taken on a new significance as people yearn for a return to normalcy and the freedom to explore new places once again. While safety concerns and travel restrictions continue to impact the industry, there is optimism that travel will rebound in the coming years, bringing with it the many benefits that it offers.

Overall, present-day travel is an important aspect of human life, providing opportunities for personal growth, cultural exchange, and economic development. It allows us to connect with others, learn from different perspectives, and broaden our understanding of the world.

Traveling can be an exhilarating experience, filled with new sights, sounds, and cultures to explore. However, for some people, the stress of travel can outweigh the enjoyment of the journey. This is where the concept of "travel and ease" comes in.

Travel has many benefits and can play an important role in personal and professional development. Some of the key benefits of travel include:

Broadening perspectives: Travel exposes individuals to new cultures, lifestyles, and ways of thinking, helping to broaden their perspectives and increase their understanding of the world.

Personal growth: Travel can challenge individuals to step outside their comfort zones, develop their independence, and gain a deeper appreciation of their own abilities and strengths.

Building relationships: Travel can provide opportunities to form new relationships and strengthen existing ones, both with friends and family and with people from different cultures.

Enhancing creativity: Travel can inspire creativity by exposing individuals to new ideas, experiences, and environments.

Improving mental and physical health: Travel has been shown to reduce stress, improve mental well-being, and increase physical activity, which can have long-lasting benefits for health and well-being.

Career development: Travel can provide opportunities for professional growth and development, including networking, learning new skills, and gaining new experiences.

In today's interconnected world, travel is more accessible and affordable than ever, and it can play an important role in helping individuals grow and develop. Whether for personal or professional reasons, travel can provide a wealth of benefits that can enrich individuals' lives and enhance their well-being.

Three illogical adjectives of our lives are "busy," "hardworking, urgent.

Busy: Nobody is ever "too busy," and if they are interested, they will make time. It's not about "having" time. It's about making time. A person being "too busy" is a myth. People make time for the things that are really important to them! No matter how busy a person is, if they really care, they will always find the time for you.

Urgent: An urgent word is often a substitute for our own delayed action. In general, the word "urgent" will have no meaning if we complete all of our work on time. If we start anything a little earlier, then unnecessary nervousness about the urgency issue could become meaningless. Overall, someone's delay becomes another person's urgent issue. Disposing of all our responsibilities in time can avoid the word "urgent," except for uninvited problems like natural calamities and untoward events.

Working Hard: The meaning of "working hard" is called into question because work should be viewed as a pleasurable and relaxing experience. When you get the feeling of working hard, it implies that you are not suited for the job, whereas others may not feel hard and may be suited to do the job with pleasure.

Work done with passion produces exceptional results, whereas work done for money does not. The need of the hour is "working smart," and traditional terms like "working tirelessly," "having extensive experience," and "working long hours" are becoming obsolete facts. The present-day demand is "street smart," meaning getting the optimum result well in time with minimum resources.

Today's requirement is about assembling the required skills and customizing them to achieve the required objectivity. The present-day style of working is not to re-invent the wheel but to enhance the existing wheel to achieve the required result.

Easy, peaceful living refers to a way of life characterized by simplicity, contentment, and a focus on the things that truly matter. It involves minimizing stress, reducing distractions, and cultivating a sense of calm and tranquility in one's daily life.

It may also involve cultivating healthy habits, such as regular exercise, a balanced diet, and adequate sleep, as well as spending time in nature and fostering meaningful relationships with others.

By embracing easy, peaceful living, individuals can improve their overall well-being and quality of life. It allows them to focus on what truly matters, reduce stress and anxiety, and cultivate a sense of gratitude and contentment in their daily lives.

Dos and Don'ts During Travel Trips

Dos:

- Plan ahead: research your destination and make a plan for your trip, including transportation, accommodations, and activities.
- Do pack appropriately; bring the necessary items for your trip, including clothing, toiletries, and any medications you may need.
- Be respectful of local customs and culture. Learn about the culture and customs of your destination and be respectful of them.

- Do stay hydrated—drink plenty of water and stay hydrated, especially in hot or humid environments.
- Do bring a first-aid kit. Bring a basic first-aid kit with essentials like bandages, pain relievers, and antiseptics.
- Do keep important documents safe. Keep your passport, tickets, and other important documents in a safe and secure place.
- Keep an open mind, be open to new experiences, and try new things while traveling.
- Do be aware of your surroundings; stay alert and aware of them, especially in unfamiliar or crowded areas.
- Do respect the environment. Be mindful of your impact on the environment and take steps to reduce your carbon footprint.
- Make memories—take photos, keep a journal, and make memories that will last a lifetime.

Don'ts:

- Don't over pack; avoid bringing too much luggage or unnecessary items that may weigh you down.
- Don't be disrespectful; avoid behaviors or actions that may be disrespectful to the local culture or customs.
- Don't ignore safety precautions; follow safety precautions, such as wearing seat belts, using helmets, or avoiding unsafe areas.
- Don't leave important items unattended. Keep an eye on your belongings and avoid leaving them unattended.
- Don't rely too heavily on technology; avoid relying solely on technology, such as your phone or GPS, and bring a physical map or guidebook as a backup.
- Don't be too rigid. Avoid being too rigid with your plans and be open to changes or unexpected opportunities.

- Don't be too trusting; be cautious around strangers and avoid putting yourself in potentially dangerous situations.
- Don't litter; avoid littering or leaving trash behind, and be mindful of the impact of your actions on the environment.
- Don't overspend; avoid overspending and stick to a budget to prevent financial stress during your trip.
- Don't forget to have fun! Remember that the purpose of your trip is to have fun and make memories, so don't forget to enjoy yourself!

“A man who dares to waste

one hour of time

has not discovered

the value of life”.

Charles Darwin

OPEN

6. Managing Life Style

Life style management involves taking intentional steps to manage your time, energy, and resources to achieve your goals and live a fulfilling life. Here are some key aspects of life management:

Lifestyle management refers to the conscious and proactive approach to managing one's habits, behavior's, and daily routines to improve health and overall well-being. It involves setting and achieving personal goals related to physical fitness, nutrition, stress management, work-life balance, and other aspects of life. The goal is to enhance the quality of life and achieve a sense of control and satisfaction in daily life. It can involve seeking the help of professionals such as health coaches, dietitians, or therapists, as well as making changes to one's environment, routines, and habits to support desired outcomes.

Time management: Prioritize your time by setting clear goals and identifying the most important tasks. Use time-management tools, such as a schedule or to-do list, to stay organized and focused.

Energy management: Manage your energy by prioritizing self-care activities, such as exercise, meditation, and adequate rest. This can help you maintain high levels of productivity and reduce stress.

Financial management: Manage your finances by setting a budget, tracking your spending, and saving for the future. This can help you achieve financial stability and reduce financial stress.

Goal-setting: Set clear and specific goals for what you want to achieve in your personal and professional lives. This can help you stay motivated and focused on your path to success.

Continuous learning: continuously learn and grow by seeking out new experiences and challenges. This can help you expand your knowledge and skills and reach your full potential.

By managing your time, energy, and resources effectively, setting clear goals, and continuously learning and growing, you can achieve success in all areas of your life and live a fulfilling and meaningful life.

Lifestyle management is the practice of adopting healthy habits and making positive changes to improve overall health and well-being. It involves making conscious

STYLE
IS NOT A
DISPLAY OF
WEALTH
BUT AN
EXPRESSION OF
IMAGINATION

decisions to live a balanced life, including taking care of our physical, mental, and emotional health.

There are various aspects of lifestyle management, including exercise, nutrition, stress management, sleep hygiene, and social connections. By focusing on each of these areas and making improvements there, individuals can reduce their risk of developing chronic diseases and improve their overall quality of life.

Exercise is an essential component of lifestyle management. Regular physical activity can help to maintain a healthy weight, reduce the risk of chronic diseases such as heart disease and diabetes, and improve mental health. Exercise also helps improve sleep quality and reduce stress levels.

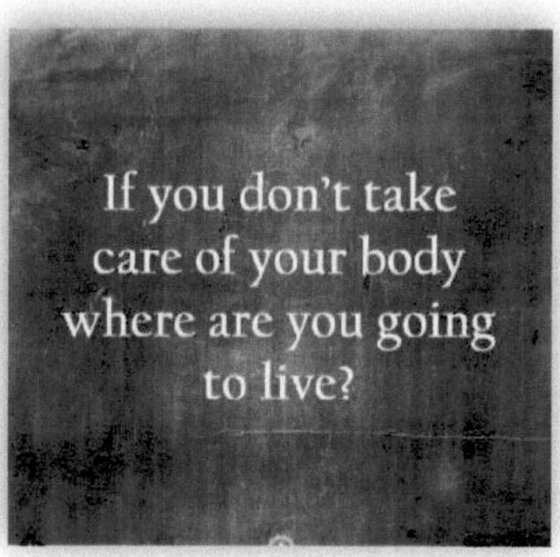

Another key aspect of lifestyle management is nutrition. A healthy diet consisting of whole foods such as fruits, vegetables, whole grains, lean protein, and healthy fats can help reduce the risk of chronic diseases and improve overall health. By reducing their intake of processed foods, sugary drinks, and unhealthy fats, individuals can improve their health and well-being.

Stress management is another essential component of lifestyle management. Chronic stress can lead to a variety of physical and mental health issues, including anxiety, depression, and heart disease. It is important to find ways to manage stress, such as by practicing mindfulness, yoga, or meditation, to promote relaxation and reduce stress levels.

Sleep hygiene is also crucial for maintaining good health. A lack of sleep can lead to a variety of health problems, including obesity, diabetes, and heart disease. Good sleep hygiene includes setting a regular sleep schedule, creating a relaxing sleep environment, and avoiding screens and other stimulating activities before bedtime.

Finally, social connections are an essential aspect of lifestyle management. Human beings are social creatures, and social connections are essential for maintaining good mental health. By creating positive social connections, individuals can reduce stress levels, improve overall happiness, and maintain good mental health.

In conclusion, lifestyle management is an essential component of maintaining good health and well-being. By adopting healthy habits and making positive changes in areas such as exercise, nutrition, stress management, sleep hygiene, and social connections, individuals can reduce their risk of developing chronic diseases and improve their overall quality of life.

One's Own Life

Finding one's own life purpose is a deeply personal and individual journey that involves introspection, self-reflection, and exploration. The purpose of life is a deeply personal and philosophical question that has been debated by philosophers, theologians, and thinkers throughout history.

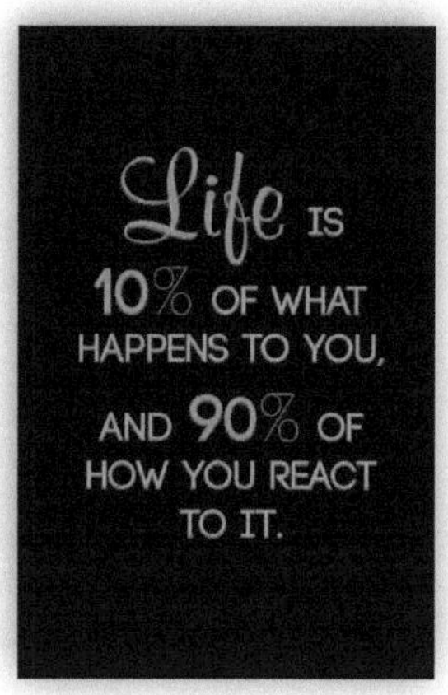

The purpose of life is a deeply personal and subjective question that can be approached from different perspectives. Whether we seek meaning, happiness, service, spiritual enlightenment, or simply to experience life, the pursuit of our own purpose can give us a sense of direction and fulfilment in our lives.

Here are some steps that may help you discover your life's purpose:

Reflect on your values: Consider what is most important to you in life, such as family, relationships, career, personal growth, spirituality, or community service. Identify your core values and what gives meaning and purpose to your life.

Explore your passions: Think about what you are passionate about and what brings you joy and fulfillment. Consider your hobbies, interests, and activities that excite you and make you feel alive.

Identify your strengths. Consider your unique strengths, talents, and abilities. What are you good at, and what do others often compliment you on?

Consider your life experiences: Your past experiences, both positive and negative, can provide valuable insights into your life goals. Consider how your past experiences have shaped your values, passions, and strengths.

Set goals and take action: Once you have identified your life's purpose, set specific goals and take action to achieve them. Break down your goals into smaller, manageable steps, and take consistent action towards them. Create your future from your future, and not from your past.

Embrace the journey: Finding your life's purpose is a journey, and it may take time and patience. Embrace the process, be open to new experiences, and stay committed to your goals.

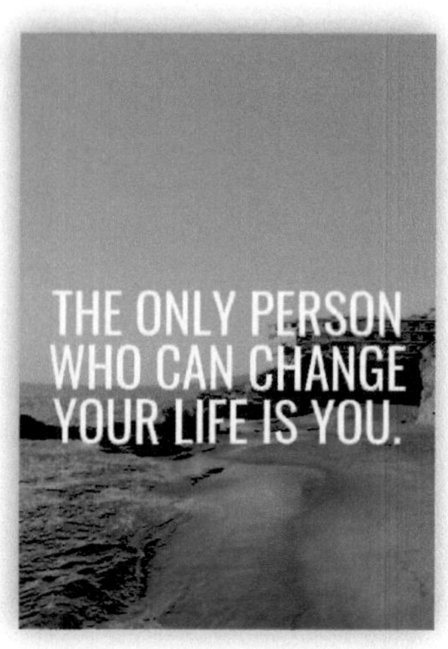

Discovering one's own life purpose is a personal and individual journey that requires self-reflection, exploration, and action. By reflecting on your values, exploring your passions, identifying your strengths, considering your life experiences, setting goals, and taking action, you can discover your life purpose and live a more fulfilling and meaningful life.

Living Simple and Thinking Big

In a world that often values material wealth and external success, it can be easy to lose sight of what truly matters in life. While achieving big goals and pursuing ambitious dreams can be important, it is equally important to live a simple and fulfilling life. By thinking big and living simply, we can create a life that is both meaningful and satisfying.

Thinking big involves setting lofty goals and working towards achieving them. It means challenging ourselves to reach beyond what we think is possible and pushing our limits. This can be a daunting process, but it can also be incredibly rewarding. When we think big, we open

---

Work until

You no longer

Have to

Introduce yourself

---

ourselves up to new possibilities and opportunities, and we can create a sense of purpose and direction in our lives.

However, thinking big does not mean losing sight of the importance of living simply. Living simply means valuing the things that truly matter in life, such as relationships, experiences, and personal growth. It means being content with what we have and finding joy in the simple pleasures of life. By living simply, we can create a sense of peace and contentment that cannot be found in material possessions or external success.

Thinking big and living simply can go hand in hand. When we pursue big goals and ambitious dreams, we must also be mindful of our values and priorities. We must ask ourselves what truly matters in life and how our goals align with those values. By living simply, we can create the space and clarity we need to pursue our goals with intention and purpose.

In a world that often values material wealth and external success, it can be easy to lose sight of what truly matters. However, by thinking big and living simply, we can create a life that is both fulfilling and meaningful. We can pursue our goals with intention and purpose while also valuing the things that truly matter in life. By finding the balance between ambition and simplicity, we can create a life that is both successful and satisfying.

Smartly Managing Money

Smartly managing money involves developing strategies and practices to make the most of your financial resources. It involves setting financial goals, creating a budget, and Starting out to make money is the greatest mistake in life tracking your income and expenses. Do what you feel you have desire for doing, the money will come. Here are some key elements of smart money management:

Set financial goals: Determine your short-term and long-term financial goals and create a plan to achieve them.

Create a budget: Create a budget that outlines your income and expenses and helps you stay on track with your financial goals.

Track expenses: Keep track of your expenses and review them regularly to identify areas where you can cut back and save money.

Manage debt: Create a plan to pay off debt, avoid taking on new debt, and manage existing debt responsibly.

Save for emergencies: Build an emergency fund to cover unexpected expenses and avoid relying on credit cards or other forms of debt.

Money should always be kept in circulation. If you hoard it for a rainy day, you will have to spend it on an ark.

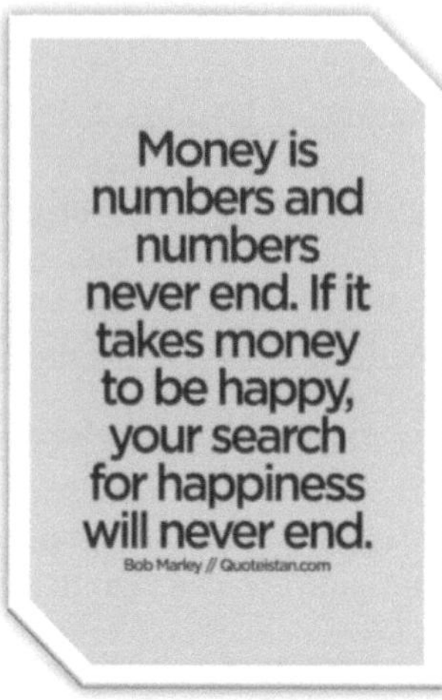

Invest for the future: Start investing for the long term to grow your wealth and achieve your financial goals.

Practice responsible spending: Avoid overspending and practice responsible spending habits, such as waiting to make purchases until you can afford them.

Smart money management is essential for achieving financial stability and long-term wealth. By making smart financial decisions and developing good money habits, you can improve your financial situation and achieve your financial goals.

Career choices: Money can be a major factor in career decisions, as it can influence job choices, salary negotiations, and overall career satisfaction. Smart money management can help you build wealth and create more flexibility in your career choices.

Relationships: Money can also be a factor in relationships, as financial stress can cause tension and conflict. By managing money effectively, you can reduce financial stress and build stronger relationships with loved ones.

Well-being: Financial stress can also impact mental and physical well-being. By managing money effectively and reducing financial stress, you can improve your overall health and well-being.

Managing your money effectively is essential for creating a fulfilling and meaningful life. By setting financial goals, creating a budget, and practicing responsible spending habits, you can improve your financial situation and achieve your life goals.

The concept of a good life is subjective and can vary from person to person depending on their individual values and beliefs. However, there are some general principles that can guide people in their pursuit of a good life.

One key aspect is having a sense of purpose or meaning in life, which can come from pursuing personal goals and passions or contributing to something larger than oneself. Another important aspect is having fulfilling relationships with family, friends, and the community, as social connections and support can greatly enhance one's well-being.

Living a healthy lifestyle through regular exercise, nutritious food, and sufficient sleep is also important for a good life, as physical and mental health are closely linked. Additionally, managing stress and cultivating positive emotions such as gratitude and joy can improve overall well-being and happiness. Get in touch with the silence within yourself and every action in life has a specific purpose.

Finally, having financial security and stability can also contribute to a good life, as it can provide a sense of freedom and the ability to pursue one's goals and aspirations. However, it's important to remember that material wealth is not the only factor in a good life and that finding balance and contentment in all areas of life is key to overall happiness and well-being.

When life hands you a lemon,

Squeeze it and make lemonade.

W Clement Stone

OPEN

7. Digitizing Life

Diligence in a digitized life refers to being responsible and mindful when using digital tools and technology in your daily life. In a digitized world, it's important to take steps to protect your personal information and well-being and to use technology in a way that enhances rather than detracts from your life.

Digital life refers to the way in which individuals interact with technology and use digital tools to communicate, work, learn, and connect with others. With the increasing prevalence of digital devices and the internet, digital life has become an integral part of modern society.

Digital life encompasses a range of activities, from using social media to stay connected with friends and family to shopping and banking online to working remotely using digital tools. While digital life has many benefits, such as increased convenience and access to information, it also

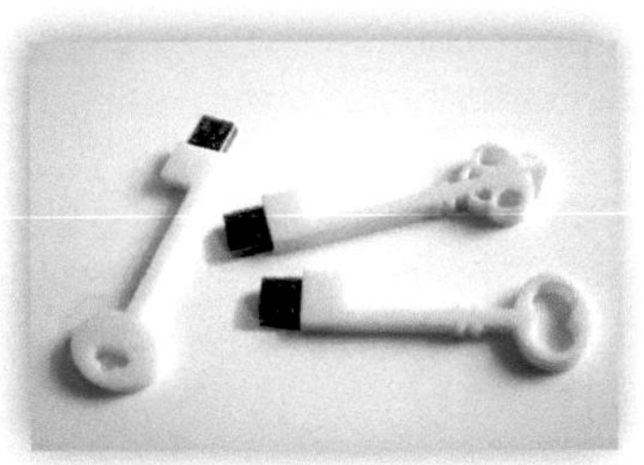

presents new challenges, such as the need to protect personal information and navigate the complex digital landscape.

To live a successful digital life, it's important to be mindful and responsible in your use of technology, to stay informed about digital trends and developments, and to take steps to protect your personal information and well-being. By embracing the opportunities and challenges of digital life, individuals can build a rich and fulfilling life in the digital age.

Here are some steps you can take to exercise diligence in a digitized life:

Protect your personal information: Be cautious about what information you share online and take steps to secure your accounts and devices.

Limit screen time: Establish boundaries for your use of technology and avoid over-reliance on screens.

Be mindful of your online behavior. Avoid engaging in negative or harmful online behavior, and be mindful of the content you consume and share.

Take care of your physical and mental well-being. Make sure to take breaks from screens and engage in activities that promote physical and mental wellness.

Stay informed: Stay informed about the latest developments in technology and digital privacy, and take steps to protect yourself and your loved ones.

By being diligent and responsible in your use of technology, you can ensure that your digital life enhances, rather than detracts from, your overall well-being and happiness.

Today's digital age has the advantage of allowing us to adopt a new safe, healthy, and enjoyable lifestyle according to our desire and budget. Now, information is the key to any success. The need of the hour is to adopt and utilize updated and reliable information and appropriate technology for our better lives. The real challenge is deciding which technology to incorporate into our daily lives based on our level of adoptability and budget. Adopting a digitally monitored lifestyle can simplify our lives. All unnecessary engagements and your physical presence for everything can be eliminated with the right technology.

Digital Technology

Digital technology has rapidly evolved in recent years and is set to continue doing so in 2023. This technology has had a significant impact on various aspects of our lives, including communication, entertainment, education, healthcare, and business.

One of the most significant advancements in digital technology is the development of artificial intelligence (AI). AI is a technology that allows machines to learn and adapt to new situations. In 2023, AI is expected to continue to revolutionize many industries, including healthcare, transportation, and finance. For instance, AI-powered healthcare systems can help doctors to diagnose diseases, personalize treatment plans, and monitor patients remotely. Self-driving cars that rely on AI technology are also becoming more common, which will help to reduce traffic accidents and improve transportation efficiency.

The Internet of Things (IoT) is another digital technology that is expected to grow significantly in 2023. IoT refers to the connection of various devices to the internet, allowing them to communicate with each other and perform specific functions. In 2023, IoT is expected to play a significant role in home automation, energy management, and transportation. For example, smart homes equipped with IoT devices can automatically adjust temperature, lighting, and security systems based on the resident's preferences and behavior. In transportation, IoT-enabled vehicles can communicate with traffic signals, other cars, and pedestrians, enabling safer and more efficient traffic flow.

Digital technology is also expected to have a significant impact on the workplace in 2023. Remote work and virtual collaboration will continue to grow in popularity, driven by technological advancements such as video conferencing, cloud computing, and collaboration tools. These technologies enable workers to communicate and collaborate with colleagues from anywhere in the world, leading to increased productivity and reduced costs.

The entertainment industry is also set to experience significant changes in 2023, driven by advancements in digital technology. Streaming services such as Netflix and Disney+ are already disrupting traditional TV broadcasting, and this trend is expected to continue in 2023. Virtual and augmented reality technology is also expected to revolutionize the gaming industry, providing players with immersive and interactive gaming experiences.

Artificial Intelligence

Artificial intelligence (AI) is rapidly evolving and transforming many aspects of our lives, including the way we work, learn, and communicate. As AI becomes more advanced, there is increasing concern about its potential impact on humans and the future of society.

One of the primary concerns is the potential for AI to replace human jobs. As AI technology becomes more sophisticated, it is capable of performing tasks that were previously done by humans, such as data analysis, customer service, and even driving. This could lead to significant job displacement, particularly in industries that rely heavily on manual labor or repetitive tasks.

However, while AI has the potential to replace some jobs, it also has the potential to create new ones. For example, as companies adopt AI technology, they will need professionals who can develop, implement, and maintain these systems. Additionally, AI could lead to the creation of new industries and markets, such as personalized medicine, self-driving cars, and smart homes.

Another concern is the potential impact of AI on human decision-making. As AI systems become more advanced, they may be able to make decisions that are faster and more accurate than humans. However, there is a risk that AI systems could reinforce existing biases and perpetuate discrimination. Therefore, it is essential to ensure that AI systems are designed with ethics and fairness in mind, and appropriate measures are in place to prevent harm.

Despite these concerns, AI has the potential to enhance human capabilities and improve the quality of life for people around the world. For example, AI-powered healthcare systems can help doctors to diagnose diseases more accurately and personalize treatment plans based on patients' individual needs. AI-powered transportation systems can reduce traffic accidents and improve transportation efficiency. AI-powered education systems can personalize learning and provide students with more individualized support.

In conclusion, AI is rapidly evolving, and it has the potential to transform many aspects of our lives. However, it is important to ensure that AI is developed and used ethically and responsibly, with appropriate measures in place to protect individuals' privacy, security, and well-being. As AI continues to evolve, it will be essential to find a balance between the potential benefits and the potential risks, and to work together to shape a future that benefits all members of society.

Digital Innovation

Digital innovation and technology have many benefits; they also have some significant drawbacks. It is important to consider these disadvantages and work to address them as we continue to innovate and develop new technologies. We must find a way to use digital technology responsibly and ethically to ensure that it benefits everyone and does not harm individuals, society, or the environment.

There are many ways to take advantage of AI and digital technology. Here are some suggestions:

Automate repetitive tasks: Look for ways to automate repetitive tasks using AI-powered tools and software. This can help you save time and increase productivity.

Personalize your approach: Use AI-powered tools to personalize your approach to customers or clients. By tailoring your approach to individual needs, you can provide a better customer experience and build stronger relationships.

Analyze data: Use AI-powered data analysis tools to gain insights into your business or industry. This can help you identify trends, spot opportunities, and make data-driven decisions.

Improve communication: Use digital technology to improve communication with colleagues, clients, and customers. Video conferencing, instant messaging, and other digital tools can help you stay connected and collaborate more effectively.

Stay informed: Keep up-to-date with the latest AI and digital technology developments in your industry. Attend conferences and training sessions, read industry publications, and stay informed about new tools and software.

Protect your data: As you take advantage of AI and digital technology, it's important to protect your data and the data of your clients or customers. Use strong passwords, keep your software up-to-date, and use security software to prevent cyberattacks.

By automating tasks, personalizing your approach, analyzing data, improving communication, staying informed, and protecting your data, you can leverage these technologies to increase productivity, provide better customer experiences, and grow your business.

Cybersecurity

With the increased use of digital technology, there is also an increased risk of cybersecurity breaches. These breaches can result in the theft of sensitive information, such as personal data and financial information.

Social isolation: The use of digital technology can lead to social isolation as people spend more time online and less time interacting with others in person.

Job displacement: Digital innovation and technology can lead to the displacement of jobs as machines and automation replace human labor. This can lead to significant job loss and economic disruption.

Overreliance on technology: As we become more dependent on technology, we may lose some of our ability to think critically and problem-solve without technology. This can lead to a lack of creativity and innovation.

Negative impact on mental health: The use of digital technology can have a negative impact on mental health, particularly among young people. Excessive use of social media, for example, can lead to anxiety, depression, and other mental health problems.

Environmental impact: The production, use, and disposal of digital technology can have a negative impact on the environment, particularly if not disposed of properly.

We live in a chaotic and haphazard era, with a high risk of cyber-crime and theft, so technological advancement

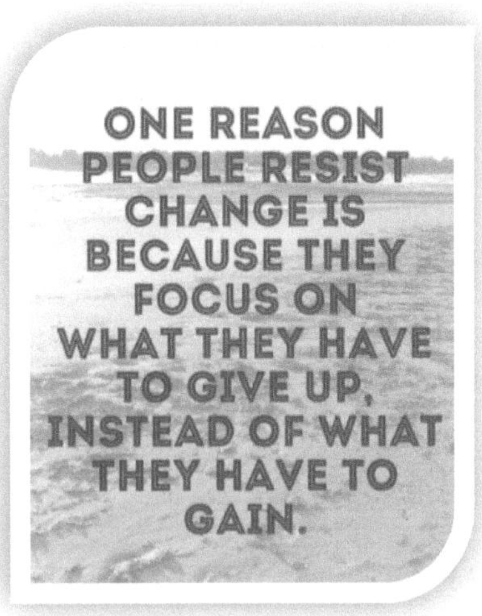

has made it easier for everyone to live their lives with proper convenience. However, you must keep in mind that the overuse of technology is not suitable for everyone, so everything should be used in moderation. Make the best use of technology and learn something practical that adds something extensive to your existing knowledge. Communication is no longer a hurdle, so take out some time for your loved ones and have effective communication with them

Digital technology is set to continue to revolutionize various aspects of our lives in future. The advancements in AI, IoT, remote work, and entertainment are just a few examples of the profound impact that digital technology will have on society. However, it is important to ensure that digital technology is used responsibly and ethically, and appropriate measures are in place to protect individuals' privacy and security.

However, while digital technology brings many benefits, it also poses significant challenges. One of the primary concerns is the impact of digital technology on privacy and security. As digital technology becomes more pervasive in our lives, it collects vast amounts of data that can be used for various purposes. Therefore, it is essential to ensure that digital technology is used ethically and responsibly, and appropriate measures are in place to protect individuals' privacy and security.

How can you use technology to ease your day-to-day life?

- Design and simplify all the hurdles in your day-to-day life by using appropriate technology and gadgets.

- You can start your day by hearing your own choice of song as a wake-up alarm on your smart phone or smart TV.

- Install an auto-cutoff sensor at your water sump and overhead tank for a continuous water supply that eliminates the need to monitor sump and water levels. By doing this, you become eco-friendly and save on your electricity bill and waste of water from overflowing water.

- Install a standard digital locker for your vital doors with multiple options of opening with a manual key, a card, or a passcode, biometrics, and an OTP for visitors with specific timings and dates.

- Install a solar system and solar lights to take care of your electricity problems.

- Install a maintenance-free power backup and connect with the Internet, security cameras, and important appliances and lights.

- Install a wireless HD camera and CCTV with record and storage for viewing, storing, and controlling from anywhere on the earth through your mobile device, and install door-break alarm sensors in all vital places.

- Installing Wi-Fi-enabled appliances, such as a TV, fridge, washing machine, fan, geyser, micro-oven, etc., for controlling and monitoring them through mobile not only saves electricity but also helps reduce environmental damage.

- Install a high-end video door phone for monitoring and interacting with visitors through your mobile device, wherever you are on the earth.

- Wear a high-end smart watch to monitor your health at all levels and at all times, and report or contact your immediate family members for any medical emergencies or untoward incidents.

- All your utility bills, like EB bills, Internet bills, telephone bills, newspaper subscriptions, mobile recharge, all your annual maintenance bills, property tax, water tax, regular fees, etc., can be automated through your bank portal's on-line instructions. All household maintenance can be automated through various portals to repair or make payments.

- You can set up all your important function dates and your kith and kin's important function dates on your mobile to remind you or to send greetings or gifts to the concerned persons.

- You can hire a reputed wealth management agency for all your money management, property dealings, leisure and travel, and all sorts of entertainment events to be managed smoothly and professionally through mobile.

- You can hire a car for short or long trips to your portals according to your budget, and you can pack and forward any of your household goods or any other goods to go anywhere through online logistic agencies through your mobile

- You can hire a medical team for home care or arrange a visit for your medical checkup at your home through your online portal.

Antifragility

Antifragility goes beyond resilience and robustness. Resilience allows one to withstand shocks while maintaining the same state, while antifragility improves under stress.

Cell phones bring you closer to the person far from you. But take you away from the ones sitting next to you.

To safeguard your mental and physical health, it's crucial to create multiple options for important decisions. Always prepare for both the best and worst-case scenarios and have a fallback plan, or a Plan B for Plan A, for critical programs. A timely fallback option can solve many problems.

To secure a steady income after retirement, it's advisable to save or deposit a small amount early in life. Digitizing critical documents such as passports, bank details, ATM cards, certificates, and medical records and storing them on cloud storage is essential. One can also send a copy to a trusted family member.

It's essential to use technology wisely, carefully, and sensibly since gadgets and technologies have their benefits and drawbacks.

To protect your online transactions and personal information, create a separate account for online transactions and set a lower limit for different categories of transactions. Transfer funds from your primary account to your online transaction account as needed. Set all transactions to pass through mobile OTPs, and configure your bank to send text and email alerts for all transactions.

Avoid using predictable passwords such as dates of birth, names, or mobile numbers. Use combinations of upper- and lower-case letters, numerical, and special characters to create meaningless words. Never keep your bank details, login information, and password details in your wallet or mobile device. Instead, keep them in a trusted email's cloud storage, which requires a password to access.

Use virtual ATM cards that require biometric touch for transactions to avoid carrying physical ATM cards or pin details. Don't count bulk cash at ATM enclosures since it can invite trouble. Finally, never reveal your KYC information through messages, links, or phone calls. Always call bank landlines to cross-check and verify.

"Growth is painful.

Change is painful.

But nothing is

as painful as

staying stuck

somewhere

you don't belong".

8. Managing Growth

Materialistic growth refers to a narrow focus on economic development and the accumulation of material possessions, often at the expense of other aspects of human well-being, such as social and environmental health. It is often associated with consumerism, where individuals are encouraged to constantly buy and consume more in order to achieve happiness and fulfillment.

In contrast, holistic growth refers to a broader perspective that encompasses multiple aspects of human well-being, including social, environmental, and spiritual health. It recognizes that true progress cannot be measured solely in terms of economic growth, but must also consider factors such as community well-being, environmental sustainability, and cultural preservation.

While materialistic growth may lead to short-term gains in economic development and individual prosperity, it can also have negative long-term consequences, such as environmental degradation, social inequality, and a lack of meaning and purpose in life. In contrast, holistic growth recognizes that human well-being is interconnected and seeks to balance economic development with social and environmental sustainability.

Ultimately, the choice between materialistic growth and holistic growth is a matter of values and priorities. By embracing a holistic perspective, individuals and societies can achieve a more sustainable and fulfilling way of life that prioritizes the well-being of all living beings and the planet we call home.

Materialistic growth is destructive where as normal or endurable or sustainable growth is constructive and helps environmental. Any form of materialistic growth is nothing more than a descent into peril. However non-materialistic growth is needed now more than ever, like human moral values like tolerance, humility, and humanity, and a happiness index instead of the GDP or any other economic index, while safeguarding all global resources and using them judiciously.

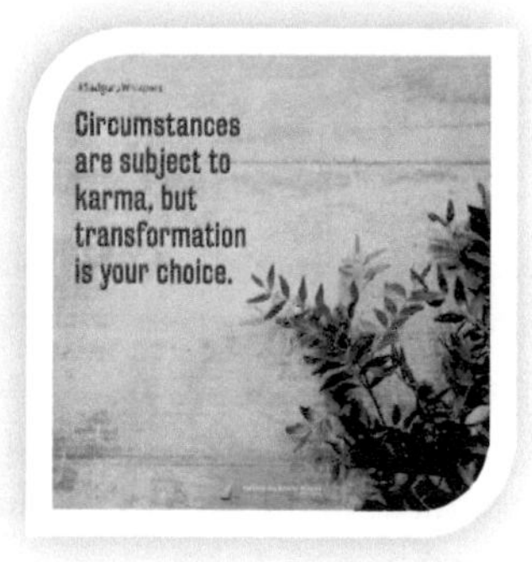

Growth tends to fill everything, leaving no room for future options. Growth saturates everything and leaves nothing for future developments. Growth forces everything into a corner and makes it immovable from there. Growth shuts down your creativity by not allowing you to use any space to let out your dreams. High growth rates, extreme standards, and the highest standards are not good for our future. Whereas normal, consistent, average, and constant are future words for our better lives.

Optimal growth may change the world order in the future, putting countries that have yet to grow and develop in a much better position than optimally grown and developed countries. Because underdeveloped or non-developed countries have unused natural resources and a clean mind and environment, they can adopt sustainability technology and other cutting-edge viable sources to suit their lifestyle. Fresh and unpolluted air allows all kinds of new experiments to be explored for a better life.

Our Mother Earth is a beautiful place to live, with all living beings living in harmony and all the resources needed for everyone to live and enjoy themselves. However, we failed to use the resources judiciously within ourselves. Resources are used in excess of their requirements and are wasted, whether knowingly or unknowingly. Recyclable resources should be used whenever possible instead of non-recyclable products. The main culprit for all the sins is "growth." In the name of growth in everything, we practically spoil the environmental aspects and use up scarce natural resources.

Growth is a Trap

We are a society that is obsessed with growth. We want things to get bigger and bigger, and we want them now. But the truth is that growth kills our space to think new and develop new things in future.

Growth can be good for your business if you're looking to expand and grow, but if you're not thinking about how this growth will affect the environment, then it's not really going to benefit anyone at all. Growth is unfriendly to nature because it takes up more space than it needs, which means fewer resources are available for other uses.

Growth kills our space to think new and develop new things in future. We are destroying ourselves with consumerism, materialism and greed.

We need to start thinking of how we can sustain our planet, because right now we are destroying it at an alarming rate!

It's important to maintain a balance between growth and preservation. We need both in order for our planet to survive. We have the tendency to think that growth is the only way to go, but in reality it's not

We believe in the power of new ideas and new ways of thinking, but we also believe in the importance of protecting our environment--and that means being careful not to kill off any part of it just because we want more space for ourselves.

It's a seductive idea, one that convinces us that we can grow and grow, and that's all we need to do. We'll be successful in life--we'll have more money and more stuff, and then we'll be happy. But this isn't true--it's an illusion. Growth is unfriendly to nature because it kills our space to think new and develop new things in future. It saturates

A seed grows
with no sound,
but a tree falls
with huge noise.
Destruction has noise,
but creation is quiet.
This is the power
of silence...
Grow Silently.

all available resources and not giving any future development or options. It kills creativity to make any new and stops us from using updated technological advantages that can help us grow further than ever before!

"Whatever makes you uncomfortable is your biggest opportunity for growth"- Bryant H. Mcgill

Sustainable Development

Therefore, the need of the hour is "sustainable development without compromising the ability of future generations to meet their own needs." Sustainability is not just environmentalism. The three pillars of sustainability are:

Environmental Sustainability: Ecological integrity is maintained; all of earth's environmental systems are kept in balance while the natural resources within them are consumed by humans at a rate at which they are able to replenish themselves.

Economic Sustainability: Human communities across the globe are able to maintain their independence and have access to the resources (financial and otherwise) that they require to meet their needs. Economic systems are intact, and activities such as secure sources of livelihood are available to everyone.

Social Sustainability: Universal human rights and basic necessities are attainable by all people who have access to enough resources in order to keep their families and communities healthy and secure. Healthy communities have just leaders who ensure personal, labor, and cultural rights are respected and all people are protected from discrimination.

Growth is Distractive

The statement "growth is distractive" suggests that personal and professional growth can present challenges and risks. While growth can lead to positive outcomes and personal fulfilment, it can also be accompanied by uncertainty, discomfort, and the potential for failure.

For example, taking on new challenges or trying new things can result in personal growth, but it can also bring about fear of failure, self-doubt, and the need to adapt to new situations and environments. It's important to recognize that growth and change are inherent parts of life and that taking risks and embracing challenges can result in personal and professional growth and fulfillment. However, it's also important to be mindful of the risks and challenges associated with growth and to be prepared to face and overcome them.

Overall, growth can be both rewarding and dangerous, and it's important to be aware of the risks and benefits and to approach growth with intentionality, awareness, and a willingness to learn and adapt.

"Today's problem is not atomic energy but man's heart. Peace can't be kept by force; it can only be achieved by understanding". – Albert Einstein.

Rarely Asked Questions

Are we fulfilling the purposes of our birth or life?

Are we conscious about to become a better person to make a better world?

Are we managed by whom?

Are we learning or experimenting with our lives?

Are we humans or money-making machines?

Are we abiding by laws and regulations?

Are we safeguarding the Earth?

Are we fulfilling the purposes of our birth or life?

It might be yes or it might be no; in fact, the real objectivity of our birth is undefined. Objectivity varies from person to person due to various aspects of their lifestyle. The objectivity of life depends on an individual's inner consciousness, which is not a constant and varies from time to time according to their own priorities. There are numerous questions that arise when attempting to determine the true objectivity of our birth, such as whether we were born to care for our parents or to care for our families or relatives, to fulfil our parents' desires, to fulfil our own desires, to care for society, to care for our country, or to care for the world in which we were born. Hence, it is a paradox to uncover the truth.

Are we conscious about to become a better person to make a better world?

Be True to Yourself: To become a better person, one must always be true to oneself. Confess the good, the bad, and the ugly and embrace it. In order to improve as a person, you first have to be really aware of who you are and who you are not.

Give Compliments: We are not saying that you should give superficial compliments, we are saying that you should really compliment someone for something they do or who they are. Lots of people want to feel valued, and this little gift will make a difference in their lives.

Help People That You Are Not Friends with: It's easy to help someone you like, but it's much more difficult to help someone you don't like. But your actions should be a reflection of you, regardless of who is asking for help. If you keep bringing forth good things in this world, it will come back to you ten times in unexpected ways.

Be Stronger Than Your Ego: The ego drives us away from being really kind and compassionate. It is our ego that tells us that we should get angry or that we shouldn't talk to someone or forgive someone. When you put your ego aside, you start to see things differently. You get less angry and notice positive changes in your life.

Put Your Negative Habits Aside: Smoking, gossiping, or judging – please don't! Give up bad habits and replace them with good ones. If you can't give up your bad habits right away, start small until you can really get rid of them.

Smile to Strangers: It's hard to be friendly when you are in a hurry, waiting in line in the grocery shop, or being squeezed on the subway. But a little smile is enough. Smiling at strangers, especially in the morning, makes the day brighter for everyone.

Surprise Someone: Surprise your friends, your partner, or your children. No matter how old we are, we all love surprises – good ones, of course. And it doesn't have to be a big gesture, sometimes a simple message, card, or letter is enough. Be creative!

Create Something Meaningful: Creating something that other people can benefit from is priceless. Whether craft or business, whether blog or book, whether special food or an entire restaurant. Keep thinking about how you can add value to your community. Create something meaningful.

Forgive and Forget: Is there a person that hurt you in the past, and you still are mad at the person or don't talk to him or her? Can we leave behind the pain or misunderstanding we associate with him or her? Can we develop compassion in any form by dealing with it?

The optimal level of truth about the objectivity of our birth, on the other hand, could be to protect our own world, where we have taken birth to experience our life for one time.

Are we safeguarding Mother Earth?

"Mother Earth, our mother earth...

She is the one who gives birth to us.

The trees, soil, mountains, and hills...

Everyone is being killed one by one.

In the forests, we hear a sweet bird's chirp.

Trees are being cut down one by one.

However, no trees are being planted on Earth.

Mother Earth, our Mother Earth...

Help us save our Mother Earth".

Forests, which cover almost 31% of the land area on our planet, play a critical role in mitigating climate change. They help produce vital oxygen and have been providing food, fresh water, clothing, traditional medicine, and shelter to many people. However, in recent times, there has been an unusual spurt of forest fires in major parts of India. Data from the Forest Survey of India shows that there has been a 65% rise in the number of forest fires nationwide. Such things have given rise to deforestation, which has become one of the factors contributing largely to global climate change too. It has contributed to 63% of the total disaster in the last 20 years. And to some extent, we human beings have played a major role by not controlling this activity.

With such incidents occurring rapidly, it is clear that we as individuals should come forward and take on the onus of protecting and safeguarding our Mother Earth. This initiative also marks a significant step taken by India towards beginning work on cutting down on greenhouse gas emissions.

As parents and responsible citizens, I believe we have the responsibility to teach our kids to care for our world. And it is much simpler than most people believe. Here are some simple tips to make a difference and help conserve Mother Earth. By: Bajaj Allianz Life

Take your family to the park and talk to them about the joy of being in green, clean, preserved places.

When you are outside, pick up your trash and teach your kids that, just as they do not litter at home, they should act the same in our "global home."

If you have a garden, please teach your kids to care for the garden. If you live in an apartment building, have potted plants and take care of them.

Have a compost bin and put your organic waste in it. Separate your garbage and recycle.

Walk, ride a bike, use public transport if you can, or car pool instead of driving.

Walk up the stairs instead of using the elevator (it will make you healthier too).

Are we managed by whom?

No one in the world can manage anyone without accepting our own brain signals. In the same way, no one can create a problem for others under any circumstances unless they knowingly or unknowingly accept our own acceptance in some form, somewhere, sometime. Instances like uninvited talk, accepting a free credit card or any form of freebie, consuming more alcohol, sugar, salt, or anything in excess Nothing comes for free, and most free things in nature have their own hidden agenda.

The brain stores a lot of information based on your exposure to the world beginning with the mutation stage at birth. Your actions and reactions are reflections of your stored brain data and its interpretation at various times. Brain management is the ultimate form of management for any outcome. Management of the soul (brain) and body serves as an alphabet for all other management. Our management education has to give more priority to mental as well as physical health, with significant weightage given to academic credits and merits. Lifestyle management is a basic necessity for anyone to excel in any form of management or governance. "Lead from the heart, not the head," as Princess Diana once said, applies to any management.

Are we learning or experimenting with our lives?

All life is an experiment. The more experiments you make, the better. The purpose of life is to live it, to taste experience to the utmost, and to reach out eagerly and without fear for newer and richer experiences. Life is a process of self-realization. We are maturing away from rationalization, fear, resistance, escape, commitment-phobia, ego-death paranoia, and profaning the scared. We move towards creativity, joy, contentment, transcendence, insight, harmony, beauty, compassion, bliss, and high power. We must conduct our experiment. We must make mistakes. We must live out our own vision of life. And there will be errors. You do not live if you avoid making mistakes. A satisfied life is better than a successful life. Because our success is measured by others, but our satisfaction is measured by our own soul, mind, and heart. Life isn't what you're given; it's what you create, what you conquer, and what you aim to achieve.

The “earth” without “art” is just “eh”.

Today’s calamities are

the results of

our uncaring of

our mother “Earth”.

9. Global Caring

"Global care" refers to the concern and responsibility that individuals and organizations have for the well-being and sustainability of the global community and the planet. This includes taking action to address global challenges such as poverty, inequality, climate change, and social injustice and working to promote global peace, stability, and prosperity.

People's responsibilities refer to the responsibilities and obligations that individuals have to themselves, their communities, and the world at large. This includes fulfilling personal and professional obligations, contributing to the well-being of others, and taking actions to address global challenges and promote global well-being.

In today's interconnected world, individuals and organizations have a responsibility to think beyond their immediate circumstances and consider the impact of their actions on the global community and the planet. By embracing their global care and people responsibilities, individuals and organizations can play a role in promoting a more equitable, sustainable, and peaceful world.

Global Warming

Global warming refers to the long-term rise in the average temperature of the Earth's climate system. It is primarily caused by the increase of greenhouse gases, such as carbon dioxide, in the atmosphere. To avoid or mitigate global warming, individuals and governments can take the following steps:

Reduce energy consumption: This can be achieved by using energy-efficient appliances, reducing vehicle usage, and reducing energy waste.

Switch to clean energy sources: Governments and individuals can support the shift towards clean energy sources such as wind, solar, and hydropower.

Promote energy-efficient transportation: Governments can promote the use of public transportation and invest in the development of electric vehicles.

Support climate-friendly policies: Governments can implement policies that encourage the reduction of greenhouse gas emissions and support the transition to a low-carbon economy.

Encourage sustainable practices: Individuals can adopt sustainable practices such as reducing waste, eating a plant-based diet, and conserving water.

Plant more trees: Trees absorb carbon dioxide and help mitigate the effects of global warming.

Support organizations working on the issue: Individuals can support organizations working to mitigate the effects of global warming, such as environmental non-profits and research institutions.

Global warming is a complex and pressing issue that requires the concerted efforts of individuals, governments, and organizations. By taking steps to reduce energy consumption, support clean energy, and promote sustainable practices, we can help mitigate the effects of global warming and create a more sustainable future.

Corporate Social Responsibility

Corporate social responsibility (CSR) is a concept that refers to the responsibility that corporations and businesses have to society and the environment. CSR encompasses a wide range of activities and initiatives that aim to promote sustainability, address social and environmental issues, and contribute to the well-being of communities and the planet.

Some examples of CSR activities include:

Environmental sustainability: reducing greenhouse gas emissions, reducing waste, and adopting eco-friendly practices. Philanthropy: donating money and resources to charitable organizations and ensuring that business practices are transparent, fair, and do not harm people or the environment

Community engagement: investing in the well-being of local communities through programs, initiatives, and partnerships

Employee well-being: promoting a healthy work-life balance and supporting employee well-being

CSR is increasingly being recognized as an important aspect of responsible business practice, and companies are expected to demonstrate their commitment to social and environmental responsibility in their operations and initiatives. By embracing CSR, companies can contribute to a more sustainable future, build trust and reputation, and enhance their relationships with stakeholders. CSR is increasingly being recognized as an important aspect of responsible business practice, and companies are expected to demonstrate their commitment to social and environmental responsibility in their operations and initiatives. By embracing CSR, companies can contribute to a more sustainable future, build trust and reputation, and enhance their relationships with stakeholders.

The climate crisis threatens to undo the last fifty years of progress in development, global health, and poverty reduction, and to further widen existing health inequalities between and within populations. It severely jeopardizes the realization of universal health coverage (UHC) in various ways, including by compounding the existing burden of disease and by exacerbating existing barriers to accessing health services, often at the times

when they are most needed. Over 930 million people, or around 12% of the world's population, spend at least 10% of their household budget to pay for health care. With the poorest people largely uninsured, health shocks and stresses already push around 100 million people into poverty every year, with the impacts of climate change worsening this trend.

Governments and corporations need to step in, but they shouldn't bear all the responsibility for making a positive environmental impact. People from all walks of life can do things each day to reduce their carbon footprint and make their routine eco-friendlier.

Becoming an environmental warrior doesn't require a superhero-like effort. Something as simple as creating a grocery shopping list or using ceramic baking pans can make a big difference.

Every individual has a role to play in preserving the Earth's environment. A positive change, no matter how small, has the ability to create a lasting ripple of change in the long run. Imagine how much of a difference we could make if every person on the planet (that is, 7 billion!) started doing their part to reduce their carbon footprint and adopt a green lifestyle! Taking baby steps and starting by adopting positive everyday habits could go a long way towards saving the environment.

Climate change is the single biggest health threat facing humanity, and health professionals worldwide are already responding to the health harms caused by this unfolding crisis. While no one is safe from these risks, the people whose health is being harmed first and worst by the climate crisis are the people who contribute least to its causes and who are least able to protect themselves and their families against it—people in low-income and disadvantaged countries and communities.

"Whatever we sow in thought, word, or deed is that which we reap". – Karma.

Our universe reflects us how we express and what we experience are concerned. If we sow love, we reap love; if we sow hate, then that is what we reap. Now what we are experiencing the hardships are results of our actions.

Earth's Survival

Humans play a critical role in the preservation of our planet. Here are some key roles that individuals can play to help protect and preserve our environment:

Reduce your carbon footprint: One of the most pressing issues confronting our planet is climate change, which is caused by greenhouse gas emissions. Individuals can help reduce their carbon footprint by taking steps such as using public transportation, biking or walking instead of driving, reducing energy consumption, and eating a plant-based diet.

Practice responsible consumption: The production and disposal of consumer goods are major contributors to environmental problems such as pollution and waste. Individuals can reduce their impact by practicing responsible consumption, such as buying products made from sustainable materials, avoiding single-use plastics, and recycling.

Support renewable energy: Switching to renewable energy sources such as solar, wind, and hydroelectric power can help reduce greenhouse gas emissions and slow the effects of climate change. Individuals can support renewable energy by installing solar panels or wind turbines, supporting policies that promote renewable energy, and advocating for a shift away from fossil fuels.

Protect natural habitats: Protecting natural habitats such as forests, wetlands, and coral reefs is critical to preserving biodiversity and combating climate change. Individuals can support efforts to protect natural habitats by volunteering, donating to environmental organizations, and advocating for policies that protect these areas.

Here are a few things you, as an individual, could start doing to make this world a much "greener" and better place.

Adopt the 3R technique: reduce, reuse, and recycle.

To begin, make every effort to reduce resource waste and domestic waste as much as possible. Buy only what you need, and it is a wise move to buy large packets (more quantity of product but less waste generated when it comes to packaging). Always reuse items that can be used more than once, such as grocery and shopping bags. Opt for washable utensils over disposable ones. indulge in recycling products to create new products.

Instead of dumping away the organic waste (vegetable and fruit peels, flowers, leaves, etc.) produced in your house daily in a landfill, try composting. Make a pit in your backyard and begin dumping organic waste into it. When the hole is filled, cover it up with soil. The organic waste will decompose in several weeks and will serve as natural manure for the soil.

Always, always remember to unplug used chargers from the sockets and switch off the lights, fans, and any other electrical appliances when not in use. You may not realize it, but these little acts of carelessness may be the reason behind your skyrocketing electricity bills. By switching off devices and appliances when not in use, you are not only cutting down on your energy costs but also saving a considerable amount of energy.

Replace the ageing and energy-hogging appliances in your home with new, energy-efficient ones. Today, the market is filled with energy-efficient bulbs, fans, heaters, air conditioners, TVs, refrigerators, and so much more. These devices deliver excellent performance while consuming minimal energy. Thus, the overall consumption of electricity in your house will reduce to a large extent, as will your utility bill.

Trees provide us with oxygen, shade, and rainfall. They are critical in combating climate change, which is engulfing the entire planet. Do your part and make it a point to plant trees in your surrounding areas. You can take the initiative during festivals or other special occasions and create a tree planting drive in your neighborhood. This way, you will encourage others to plant trees for a greener future.

Try to avoid driving and use public transportation. Individual cars and automobiles not only increase overall fuel consumption but also contribute to daily air pollution. By riding public buses, trains, metros, etc., you can help reduce this. Choose e-receipts and bills over paper bills. This will help save our forest resources.

Fix any leaks and cracks in the pipes, taps, and water-cooling system in your homes. Every drop of water is precious. Adopt rainwater harvesting. By collecting rainwater in clean containers or tanks, you can create an extra buffer of water for fulfilling your domestic purposes (washing cars, watering plants, etc.). Say no to plastic

Caring for your own health is nothing more than caring for the health of others, which allows you to live in a safe and healthy world. It not only helps the environment, but it also helps healthcare environments. Healthy people are eco-friendly people because they are not burdening others with health-related waste, which includes money, hazardous waste, manpower, and many related materials. One unhealthy man is in need of assistance and care from many people around him.

Whenever and wherever you get a chance, please walk or cycle to the places you want to go and use public transport if available. Walk short distances or within a 3 km radius whenever you get the opportunity to walk instead of waiting for transport.

Well-organized multi-purpose shopping with family members, such as sorted item list for purchase, social visits, budget, target shops, location's proper routes, and choosing lean traffic time. Importance of Public transports, Walking or cycling, pooling system, Reuse, Recycle, Reduce

Patronize public transportation to encourage commuters. Utility-based automated road tax to avoid unnecessary movements of private vehicles. Banning all plastic products, particularly heavily taxing or hiking plastic bottled water

Penalize or stop free health care or any incentives or privileges for those who invite diseases by knowingly indulging unhealthy habits like drug and alcohol abuse, smoking abuse, and other abnormal activities.

Governments and non-governmental organizations (NGOs) must support all possible production methods, emphasizing the importance of recycling and reusable products through massive awareness campaigns and marketing recycle products or subsidized reusable products. Governments and NGOs can distribute reusable products like reusable water containers and shopping bags, etc., free of charge to unaffordable people through the public distribution system.

Social awareness, inclusion in the academic curriculum, a waste control and prevention body, and a watchdog committee at all levels of governance

Why we need action: Climate change is now affecting every country on every continent. It is disrupting national economies and affecting lives, costing people, communities, and countries dearly today and even more tomorrow. People are experiencing the significant impacts of climate change, which include changing weather patterns, rising sea levels, and more extreme weather events. The greenhouse gas emissions from human activities are driving climate change and will continue to rise. They are now at their highest levels in history. Without action, the world's average surface temperature is projected to rise over the 21st century and is likely to surpass 3 degrees Celsius this century—with some areas of the world expected to warm even more. The poorest and most vulnerable people are being affected the most.

Preventing global warming requires a collective effort from individuals, businesses, and governments. By taking steps to reduce greenhouse gas emissions and promoting sustainable practices, we can help mitigate the most severe impacts of climate change and create a more livable planet for ourselves and future generations.

www.ingramcontent.com/pod-product-compliance
Ingram Content Group UK Ltd.
Pitfield, Milton Keynes, MK11 3LW, UK
UKHW041955190726
13854UKWH00005B/1985

9 798890 261069